RAIN, WIND, THUNDER, FIRE, DAUGHTER

Rain, Wind, Thunder, Fire, Daughter

POEMS

H. G. Dierdorff

UNIVERSITY OF NEVADA PRESS | *Reno & Las Vegas*

University of Nevada Press | Reno, Nevada 89557 USA
www.unpress.nevada.edu
Copyright © 2024 by University of Nevada Press

Manufactured in the United States of America

FIRST PRINTING

Cover design by Caroline Dickens
Cover illustration by Naomi Kim

LIBRARY OF CONGRESS CATALOGING-IN-PUBLICATION DATA
Names: Dierdorff, H. G. (Hannah Grace), 1997– author.
Title: Rain, wind, thunder, fire, daughter : poems / H. G. Dierdorff.
Other titles: Test site poetry series.
Description: Reno, Nevada : University of Nevada Press, [2024] | Series: Test site poetry
series | Summary: "*Rain, Wind, Thunder, Fire, Daughter* narrates the speaker's coming of
age in a world of accelerating climate apocalypses and environmental loss. Throughout the
book, as the speaker deconstructs her inherited Christian fundamentalism, her worldview
and use of poetic forms expand. Written across time but in a continuous present tense, the
poems return again and again to the landscape of Eastern Washington, using rhetoric and
repetition to expose the violent legacies of patriarchy, settler-colonialism, manifest destiny,
and fire suppression."—Provided by publisher.
Identifiers: LCCN 2024011473 | ISBN 9781647791711 (paperback) | ISBN 9781647791728
(ebook)
Subjects: LCGFT: Poetry.
Classification: LCC PS3604.I22538 R35 2024 | DDC 811/.6—dc23/eng/20240329

LC record available at https://lccn.loc.gov/2024011473

For my mother

"But every age has its ghosts, a kind of rage. / The language."

—Allison Cobb, *Green-Wood*

Contents

RAIN, WIND, THUNDER, FIRE, DAUGHTER

Invoke | Revoke

Sing me [muse] another myth, another statistic
sheltering the cult of objectivity. Knowledge
without intimacy just a bird's eye view before
the bomb drops. One nation under [a sterile
claim]. Consider landscape: the Columbia
Basin. Consider the wildland-urban interface:
the zone most at risk for human ignition.
Consider population density, how Idaho differs
from Washington, the intermountain from
the coast. How causality shifts when distance
is crossed, when the POV descends to the dry
fescue grass. I want you to touch the fire
sparking from my lips or watch lightning spear
a pine snag and ask the wind to match a word
to the action: accident, judgement, arson.

As the West Coast Burns (I)

i scatter pleasure around the apartment. i gather the hair of my animal. i exhaust and wash myself. i eat.

Here is the bread, the cup, the egg. Here is my arm, my hand, lifting. See how pleasantly the tine of the fork scrapes against the plate. See how i exhume and expunge each day. See how i play make-believe. These rooms are as small as the future: cut open, cut off, staged with mass-produced props.

A knife balances on the empty plate balanced on my knee, its shape like a circle of hell. Where is it coming from, this cold, high-pitched ring?

All this show-and-tell of the self while coal blows cool air on my face, flicks flame into a lamp on command.

*

On command, the first boy i kissed evacuates Salem, drives up I-5 with his wife and son. i want to ask him about the rusted merry-go-round we found in the forest. Does his stomach still roil, a whirlpool behind his ears, the pines blurring into a bowl of light?

Tonight i am cold metal against a fingernail, a rust flake staining a palm. i am the sky after the spinning, tennis shoes and dead needles, the ground lurching like my mother's voice on the phone when she reads me my words from three years ago. She says she knows me, she knows, she knows.

*

i burn toast. i smoke. i alarm. i slice the circle of 7 am with my red repetition. i i i i i i i i i i i i i i i i i i i i i i i i i i i i i i i i i i i i i i i i i i i i i i i i. All these candles igniting the air, a forest fire there? there? there?

i remember the dead doe we found near the river. i and the boy and the others. Her hind foot snapped from leaping the chain-link. Her womb torn open by teeth. Mist shivered among the ponderosa pines. i looked at the fawn curled, exposed in the morning light, and didn't cry.

*

One night, my brother sends me a photo of Portland cloaked in smoke. My father wakes with a migraine in Spokane. Across the country, i wake, sheets flecked with flea blood and feces. The black commas of their bodies. They are dying. They curl, crawl. They drag their abdomens across my legs. i smear them onto the white page, , ,,, , , , , ,,, ,, , , ,,,,,   ,   ,   ,   ,   ,

*

i don't think of praying. Not when my mother quotes 2 Chronicles 7:14. Not when my friend texts me from San Francisco that she can't sleep, the syntax of fire a dark sliver in her side.

When i lied, my mother or father would take a wooden spoon or cut two feet from the weeping cherry as i waited in the bathroom, a hornet's nest inside. *If my people who are called by my name humble themselves, and pray and seek my face and turn from their wicked ways . . .* A child learns through the body's pain. Touch a coal to not crawl into the fireplace.

*

i brush the blister on my inner arm, the oblong inch of raised tissue where i pressed my skin to the baking pan. How i fear the healing, the blank sea where the body will erase all signs of fire, leaving only desire and distance.

Genesis

Begin with my body, with the memory
of my sister crying in the top bunk
all those nights she wakes dreaming of fire,
the house on fire, *ecology* from the Greek
oikos, meaning house or home, my home
on Normandie Lane, a name I don't know
yet as invasion, the world at war. Begin
on the street where I find myself nights
my sister's dreams drop like needles, piling
the floor with ground fuel. Begin in the dream
where I stand on the asphalt in the cold,
wrapped in Noah's ark, watching the flames engulf
the second story, the square pane of my window
shattering behind the branches of the pine.

A Power Comes Up Between the Voices

The pine is—*quiet. For Adam was formed first*
then Eve—a pine, a descendant of the ponderosa
communities that replace steppe sagebrush
around 4,000 years ago, 7,000 years after the ancestors
of the Salish cross a land bridge from Siberia, migrate
south as the ice sheet gives way to juniper and spruce.
15,000 years ago, ice damming the Clark-Fork river
ruptures, releasing glacial water east, ripping
loess and sediment from the Columbia River Basin,
carving the basalt that forms from a series of lava flows
beginning 17 million years ago. 180 million
years ago, volcanic islands collide and fuse
with the coastline near Spokane where ocean looms—
once unparsed, pre-pacific, not woman, not man.

Sonnet Two Blocks from a Strip Mall

My brother squats beside the pond overhung
by the maple's flat asterisks. His grubby fingers
lift a stone. He wants to know what's underneath.
He's five. I'm three. Love reaches my hand
into the stone's shadow to touch the damp
loam wriggling with worms and centipedes.
What's underneath? In ponderosa forests,
fungi penetrate and sheathe tree roots, the cell
walls interlacing, almost indistinguishable.
The tree receives nitrogen and water, feeds
the fungi sugar hummed from the sun. What's
underneath? A history of fire suppression,
animal grazing, urbanization, logging. Above,
my brother and I walk with dirty bare feet.

The Poet Wanders Between Memory and Dream

I'm under the pine, barefoot in the bark bed
littered with dead needles, with three-fingered
fascicles that prick my heels when I run
and hide. I enter the house my father builds
in the ponderosa, climb the branches he trims
and cuts into rough rungs. I'm asleep
on the platform circling the tree, my head
thirty feet above the earth, my ears washed
as wind lifts and drops the limbs like flotsam—
I look and see the twisted branches shiver
at the start of summer as dogs repeat the sounds
to close the day and powerlines sway and droop
over the neighborhood, their dark threads
slicing through a mosaic of stars.

Eve Speaks of Her American Childhood

Of course there are stars and stripes hung
outside the church. Tucked beside the Little
Spokane, we sing *Onward Christian Soldier*
and chase each other among the pines. Here
I kiss a boy on the plastic slide, kiss him
when the preschool teacher tells me to stop,
kiss him with soft quick pecks he doesn't remember
years later when we trace a ponderosa's dark
fissures. He peels off a jagged piece of bark
like rind from an orange, lifts it to his lips,
nibbles the edges, mouth blooming with brown
and red splinters, the wood wet with his spit,
eyes alight with pleasure. I can't remember
if I take a bite when he tells me, *here, try.*

A Poem Changes Nothing

1889. Firemen try to douse
the grease fire across the street from the depot,
but the hose won't fill, the superintendent away
working on his steamboat. The blaze races
through pine-board banks and saloons, consumes
thirty-two blocks before throwing itself
against the river's shoulder. In my coloring book,
the flames still wait for the red of a crayon,
history blank and bordered by black lines.
Absent: the fires Colonel Wright ignites
in lodges and food supplies after the Battle
of the Spokane Plains. Absent: the 600 horses
he shoots. Absent: the names of the Yakima
and Palouse he strangles and hangs near Latah Creek.

Sonnet Ending in People's Park

A story of fire is the story of Latah Creek,
how a white man coins the name by taking
two Nez Perce words, by splicing *pine* and the *stone*
pestles used to grind flour from camas roots
(those blue flowers growing in meadows once
kept open by fire, by cool burns lit in the fall
to clean and feed the land). A story of fire
is a story of a double name, the state
and nation debating *Latah* or *Hangman*, the creek
emptied of trout, turbid with manure and algae
blooms, the golden fields of the Palouse oozing
pollutants downstream to where I walk past
a shopping cart and watch a woman lean
against a cement pillar graffitied *DRUG CREEK*.

Wood | Word

Ponderosa: the jigsaw pillars that invoke
a *spiritual feeling*, pillars evolved to survive
surface fires, their lower limbs dropped with age.
Ponderosa: the name a Scottish botanist gives
the pine while botanizing along the Spokane
River in 1826. Ponderosa: in Latin, heavy,
weighty, significant. *The Latin name became—*
unusually among trees—the common name. Ponder-
osa: the tree of many names: long-leafed
pine, pumpkin, yellowbelly, bull pine, black-
jack, red pine, silver pine, pino real (true
pine). Ponderosa: ponderous: *meditative,*
labored, profound, slow because of great weight,
like a book pinning the pen in place.

The Summer Before My Baptism,
We Go Backpacking in Eastern Oregon

My father teaches the good book:
how to hook and land a rainbow trout
in the Wallowas, how to pound the head
with a rock and still the shuddering gills.
To kill and eat feels holy, life flying
out of sight like the boomerang my brother loses
in the pines. That night, paper, kindling, a match
to write a warmth we huddle around, breathing
smoke and stories. O, I will never believe
more in love than in my father's hands
cooking beans over a small blue flame, pointing
at the Milky Way or pouring creek water
on the coals. Inside the tent, we hold his voice
and believe in talking raccoons and walking trees.

Animalia

the kingdom of   [   ]   is like a man carrying
a village of animals in the trunk of his sedan—
goats, chickens, a Shetland pony from the farm in eastern
Oregon where he's always six, watching his father leave

the kingdom of   [   ]   is like a woman with no
middle name, her punctuated *W* a tattoo of the house
of wolves where her father slurs into the night,
where she hears her mother's cry sharp as canines

the kingdom of   [   ]   belongs to the children
born under this taxonomy, *Dierdorff* meaning village
of animals, a village within the realm where the children
play at survival, pick clusters from Oregon grape, make

believe horses, dogs, & dragons before being called
inside to memorize *Our Father who art in heaven*

Rain, Wind, Thunder, Fire, Daughter

Inside my body, the doll house floating
on the coffee table. My father kneels
to place a wooden girl in a cutaway
room. *Obeying God is like living under*
a roof, he says. *There's safety, shelter. Sin*
is when we step outside. He moves the doll
onto the open brown field stacked with books
and Bibles. *What will happen when a storm*
hits? Fists of lightning pummel the northwest
every summer. "Now a little fire . . . here
comes a walking fire." The roof is red.
Nearly 85% of wildland fires are human.
Outside, the seconds between light and sound
unravel whether or not God counts them.

As the West Coast Burns (II)

i run, counting the miles.

i run

> 2645 miles from the Pearl Hill Fire, 2660 miles from the Cold
> Springs Fire, 2728 miles from the Claremont-Bear fire, 2,747
> miles from the Holiday Farm Fire, 2776 miles from the Beachie
> Creek Fire, 2784 miles from the Glass Fire, 2804 miles from the
> August Complex.

Where: a wood at the edge of a -ville, the clay red with oxidized iron.

When: a humid afternoon at the tail-end of a summer of grief.

An overhanging branch scrapes skin, blood dripping a
lowercase *l* down my cheek. Before i pull out my phone to read my
face, i've already translated the pain:
> *l* for *listen up!*
> *l* for *leave*

*

i write and rewrite a poem: ~~The first time I got drunk was at Cannon Beach~~. *You must navigate the telling of your first intoxication (was it / the fire or the sea)*

Pronoun: a word in place of a ~~noun~~ confession. "You" a moniker for i/
me. The past in place of the present's abyss. A myth in place of my news
feed.

*

i read, *Human activity causes the majority of wildfires*, but lightning was
responsible for 71 percent of the area burned between 1992 and 2015.

*We want to personify these fires. We want to blame somebody. But
lightning doesn't have a face.*

In 1965, Johnny Cash set off a wildfire in Los Padres National Forest with his overheated truck, the ensuing blaze killing 49 of the area's 53 endangered condors. Responding to legal investigators, Cash said, "I don't care about your damn yellow buzzards."

In 2014, a thirteen-year-old girl set her backyard on fire in San Marcos *to see what would happen.* An ember sparked the Cocos Fire nearly half a mile away, eventually destroying 36 homes.

In 2017, a fifteen-year-old boy lobbed a smoke bomb into Eagle Creek Canyon during a fire ban. Winds blew smoke and ash west onto Portland. After three months, the fire had consumed nearly 50,000 acres along the Columbia River Gorge.

In 2018, i broke a fire ban with my friends at Cannon Beach. It was the summer before the firestorm destroyed Paradise, the summer headlines read "Portland Breaks Record for Most Days Above 90 Degrees."

*

By the end of the century, if humanity doesn't slash greenhouse gas emissions to fight climate change, "we might expect to get 50 percent more lightning."

Even if there were no changes in lightning frequency, the impact of warmer and drier conditions associated with climate change help make lightning more effective at igniting wildfires.

*

In both drafts of the poem, *a blue bottle of vodka* and *wildfires to the south and east.*

The new version ends, half accusation, half confession: *you don't talk about love (the boy who wanted / the fire, the flick of the lighter, the clean blade of liquor / cutting your throat) you say "I lit the fire I put it out"*

While i change commas and pronouns, my friend's family cabin burns down in the forest east of Salem. The forest that used to drip with old-man's beard next to the river where our faces beam in a photo from five years ago, my hair still short, our cheeks touching.

*

What remains? My memory of the parable where the man in hell cries for water. Just a fingertip dipped in a stream to cool his tongue. But it's impossible, the chasm too great to cross.

No one able to come or leave. Over 2,500 miles. All this space between.

The Poet Learns About Particle Physics

There's always a space between what exists
and what we see. Mirrors are windows inward.
I am my own council of men in clerical robes
choosing the words to make you believe a story
with margins of smoke. My action: seduction,
sedition. A repetition to replace the rhythms
of battle hymns and catechisms. Even time's
a pane of glass we manufacture and name
while outside the electrons kiss, coming
together and apart, all these flashes we read
as death, a field of particles where we fall
away. How should I translate this storm?
An electric current surges from the earth
looking to the eye like a bolt from heaven.

Prophet | Profit

Heaven is a blessed fire insurance,

the assurance of mansions after a gas leak,

after the department of men in masks and boots

watches the roof collapse, the canopy swarmed

by a hive of bees. I see red, bleed red, drink red

when my father reads *and a third of the earth*

was burned up, and a third of the trees. But the saints

will be given clean rivers, gold cities, a new

earth, a free exchange with 100% satisfaction

guarantee. No questions asked. Only purchase

this limited time offer for three payments

of $9.99! Only repeat what

the good Lord prints in neat permanent script.

Sonnet with a Mouth Full of Dollar Bills

Economy: *the production and consumption of goods
and services and the supply of money* as in "Ponderosa
pine fuel[s] the economies of the West beginning
in the 1860s." Economy: *the proper management
of the body, diet, regimen* (obsolete). At thirteen,
I exchange spaghetti for celery, cereal for the belly's
bright ache. Economy: *a sparing or careful use.*
Railroads induce clearcutting. I dream of cutting
flesh from bones, pelvis, femur, clavicle, rib cage,
breasts and sex erased as the red numbers blink
down: 130 to 108. Economy: *relating to the inter-
dependence of living things.* How the mothers praise
my body—straight, pale, and clean as the logs
laid at the lumber mill north of Coeur d'Alene.

Mapping the Channeled Scablands

South of the dam, a seven-day creation
colonizes the literal. Evolution a myth
my brother and I are taught from across
the canyon. In the campground, a boy pulls
blue tails off skinks, the survivors sun-
bathe on glacial boulders or scurry into
sagebrush. Older boys play war with broken
sticks. My brother whittles. I knit something
without shape as we debate Adam and Eve—
what's yarn or history. Every man tells me
the human story is a story of borders
and lines. All night I throw stones at a man-
made lake. Ripples of sound radiate from
the page to read the land's curves and braids.

A Ponderosa Pine Reader

A is for *androgyny*, the male & female cones growing on a single tree.

B is for *butterscotch*, the sweet vanilla scent of sun-warmed resin.

C is for *cambium*, the white inner bark rich in carbohydrates & vitamin C, harvested in the spring by the Kootenai, Colville, & Coeur d'Alene tribes, the sap layer stripped by the women, then dried.

D is for *dendrochronology*, for the history written in concentric rings radiating from the heartwood.

E is for *ectomycorrhizae*, the net of fungal filaments latticing the long-reaching roots.

F is for *fire*, for the fires lit by lightning or careful hands, fire cleaning the understory of debris & seedlings, keeping the forest open, a parkland of old growth where elk & deer gather to eat snowberry & bitterbrush leaves.

G is for the *grass*, the native grasses green & golden under the pines, for pine grass & bluebunch wheatgrass, for Idaho fescue, blue gama, & elk sedge.

H is for *heliocentrism*, for the ponderosa's fixation on the sun, its intolerance to shade.

I is for *insects*, for the pine beetles that feed on injured or diseased trees, mating in the mazes they weave between bark and sapwood.

J is for *jigsaw*, for the puzzle-pieces, the thick bark plates that shield cell growth from surface fires.

K is for *keystone species*, for the birds excavating cavities in snags, for the white-headed woodpecker, for Williamson's sapsucker, for Lewis's woodpecker, their beaks opening nests for the pygmy nuthatch & the flammulated owl.

L is for *Lewis & Clark*, for their trip down the Clearwater in dugout canoes carved from burnt ponderosa logs.

M is for *money*, for the mathematics where *A* through *K* are clearcut, crowded out, over-grazed, relocated, replaced with asphalt, banks, cheatgrass, developments, & electric fence.

N is for the *Nevada Test Site*, for the 145 ponderosas cut down & moved to Area 5, for the nuclear blast in 1953, the trees burnt & toppled like bowling pins.

A Classical Christian Academy

They shall be called oaks of righteousness, a planting of
the Lord for the display of his splendor. Isaiah 6:13

The school steals the name of a tree not found
this close to Idaho. *Quercus garryana* only grows
west of the Cascades, prefers the disturbed soil
of a post-fire landscape. No fire burns here
in the off-white halls where teachers measure
inches between plaid skirts and knees. We read
Huckleberry Finn and never learn the word *racism*,
the day's question in cursive on the board:

How does Huck exemplify Christ? Praise the Lord
whose dominion extends over algebra, art, and
history. Before manifest destiny, indigenous tribes
ignite grasslands to nurture oaks, bracken ferns,
and chocolate lilies. Each morning, I cry behind
a bathroom stall, return down the clean corridor,
black heels clicking on the stone floor. The door
opens and closes. I take my seat. The class:

apologetics. Let us evaluate our every experience
in light of God's truth. Let us critique a video
of a man who loves men as he stands at a pulpit,
tears salting his teeth. Since the 1850s, over
90% of white oak woodlands have been erased,
habitats replaced with cul-de-sacs and farms
of Christmas trees. To Christ, I pray the words
submission and *humility*. I watch my body more

than they watch me. The absence of fire never
means eternal life. Douglas firs invade, shut out
the sun, oak limbs dying in the shade where we
eat Scripture, our throats tight behind our teeth.

I Place My Mother in a Scripture

of wildflowers and burnt pines. The mountain-
side a mosaic of lupine, larkspur, and fireweed.
Among the black bare trees she stands, hands
lifting an Indian paintbrush to her face, reading
the red bracts as tongues of flame divided
by a violent wind and longing for the other
language, the locked room where touch is sight,
the body believed. Indian paintbrush, or prairie

fire, is hemiparasitic, meaning it penetrates
the roots of a host to steal water and nutrients
the way I once nursed from her body. The Navajo
use the flower as a contraceptive or to decrease
the menstrual cycle. I'm eleven when
I bleed. She opens her purse to save me.

Phonics

What opens those hours in the blue room,
my small body on my mother's lap,

her body rooted to the floor? Before the picture
books—the woman pouring oil from the still full

flask, the men standing in a circle with flames
above their heads—there is only the light's geometry

cast on carpet and the clusters of sounds in columns
down a page. /ou/ /u/ /ow/ /ai/ Grace gilding

our tongues with nonsense, a chain of light
synthesizing symbol to sound. Music grows

from the ground, tangles the lungs. Shoot, leaf,
pistil, stamen. Before I close myself in story,

this warmth passing between us like electrons
from one molecule to another, two centers

briefly linked.

As the West Coast Burns (III)

i click on a headline from the *Spokesman-Review*: "Eastern Washington slammed by fires, dust storms, and power outages." At the top, a photograph of a wheat field under a sky mottled with smoke. A lone ponderosa, two telephone poles.

On the horizon, fire shimmers in the shape of a doorway.

*

When my mother and i drove across the country, i told her i'd always wanted to write an American Odyssey but with female protagonists. Like *On the Road* but without the sexism, i almost said, but she wouldn't have known the reference and doesn't believe that word. Instead, i spun our epic: mother and daughter in the middle of winter, driving an old Toyota toward what meteorologists were calling *battleground weather*, a cold front clashing with unseasonable heat.

Was this before or after she hit the patch of ice at 70 mph? Middle-of-nowhere Montana, the divided road licked by drifting snow. i grabbed the wheel as the Avalon slalomed—*Let go!*

Before the cemetery in South Dakota, before the stories about her father, before the jackknifed semis in Iowa, the shells of sedans on the shoulder, before the hotel next to the Gentleman's Club where we holed up from the storm, i told her as we left the plateaus and mountains of dry pine, *Imagine the stories we'll tell. Men do this kind of thing all the time. Aren't we as capable, as free?*

*

A memory like a house temporarily spared from flames. An invisible threshold waits for someone's body to be carried across.

Will the fire jump the ridge, the river? Have you packed the necessities just in case?

My cat bats the pen from my fingers. A message: *stop making yourself the center of everything.*

*

Select all squares with ~~cars~~ houses.

Select all squares with ~~trees~~ bodies.

Click "continue" after the checkmark appears, verifying you're not a sequence of code programmed to navigate the web's unfathomable seas.

Look! i am human. i see pattern. i identify difference, distance, similarity. If i remove myself from each image, can i purify meaning? Look! i can refuse to enter the narrative lurking beneath the screen.

(Does this qualify as writing?)

*

In the *Spokesman-Review*, a woman watches the fire across the Okanogan River and worries. *The sky was red and the moon was up.*

Across the country, i worry, a woman, still believing if i suffer someone else can be saved. The word *across* from *o cros*: in the shape of a cross. At what age did i realize, the only way for a girl to gain power is through piety and suffering? How well i became everything they asked: rational, compliant, chaste, clean. How i sought to be a little christ, mirroring what men told me of sacrifice.

Even in the midst of environmental disaster, i can't believe my pain unless it's holy. How do i trust my words unless they embody a truth that transcends me? Oh the meanings i could reap if i wrote, *i sleep with my arms extended and my feet pressed together, a nocturnal crucifix.*

A draft in the room. Two voices, one gentle, one mocking: *Stop making your suffering more than it is.*

*

i watch myself in my father's house (the house cut in two) as windows shatter, wind scrapes scabs of shingles from the roof. The house sways in a desert spiderwebbed with cracks like a piece of sandstone about to shatter under a hammer's fist.

i dream this.

i dream a muted apocalypse, my mother's name eclipsed in my mouth. i dream a landfill in the grave of a lake—microwaves, empty Gatorade bottles, the bulbous head of a baby doll. i dream an earthquake in eastern Washington: the elephantine bones of the house explode behind us as we escape.

i carry seven words to keep my family alive.

[   ]   [   ]   [   ]   [   ]   [   ]   [   ]   [   ]

In this version of the dream, the helicopter doesn't arrive.

*

When the jet stream broadcasts smoke across the continent, i step outside, the sun engorged, familiar, pink as an infected wound.

i climb a tree by the river. A rope hangs over undisturbed water.

Double Sonnet with My Shirt Off

To assess a fire, define mortality
for the forest's basal area, *the area*
in square feet at the cross-section at breast
height of a single tree. See the tangerine

walls bleeding around the mirror where
my sister and I compare our teenage breasts,
perplexed by these new signs of likeness
and difference—the blue-green veins and dusty-

pink nipples, the size, the shape, the weight of fat
hanging over the ribcage, each breast its own
iteration of earth's atomic speech. O see

the women directed to stand beside the pines,
their breasts pendulous as plastic bags or firm
as rubber, breasts pointing to every star

on the compass, breasts purple, pitch, or parakeet
green, chests zipped shut with scars, with heavy dashes
where breasts once "O"ed the world open, ballooned
with milk or held in the mouth of love, breasts off-

centered, oblong, amorphic, breasts like two
barely raised dots read by moving the hand
across a page, breasts with faces bent or raised
like nuns toward the unseen, breasts like

snippers, their gaze level, each nipple an eye,
a scope through which the body aims. See
the foresters mark where the tissue meets

the rash-red bark, see the machine calculate
the meeting and print basal, blazon,
a blaze on the USDA report page.

Bridal | Bridle

Weekly Report from the Purity Movement:
Another daughter married at 19.
For it is better to marry than to burn
and so on. I read *Created to be His Help-*
mate and learn the male words: erection,
masturbation, arousal. In church, the girl
is glaciated in the stiff white dress. They light
the unity candle. The man receives her vow
to obey till death. Submission the final fire
suppressant, the fairytale guided to its pre-
determined denouement: the flame snuffed
before the body flares into its own white heat.
You know how Cinderella got her name.
The girl sent into smoldering coals to clean.

A Feminist Field Guide

among: of the local relation of a ~~thing~~ girl
to several surrounding ~~objects~~ beings
from the old english *in the crowd or company of*

among bobcat big-eared bat muskrat moose
chipmunk striped skunk rock chuck raccoon
cottontail black bear cougar snowshoe hare
meadow vole gray wolf mule deer masked shrew

among deer fly horse fly paper wasp hobo
swallowtail jewelwing praying mantis painted lady
pine beetle pine borer boxelder black widow
western white cabbage white twice-stabbed lady

among rainbow trout stickleback black crappie
largemouth bass bluegill brown bullhead pumpkinseed
mountain sucker whitefish walleye white crappie
(chinook and coho gone after the dam at grand coulee)

among western garter snake western skink american bullfrog
among great basin spadefoot among columbia spotted frog
among painted turtle rattlesnake northern leopard frog
among western tiger salamander among pacific tree frog

among western skink western bluebird golden eagle pacific loon
among cliff swallow violet-green swallow great blue heron canadian
    goose
among yellow warbler red-winged blackbird wood duck rock wren
among hermit thrush peregrine nighthawk kestrel merlin

~~cooper's~~ hawk among ~~swainson's~~ hawk among ~~swainson's~~ thrush among
    ~~lincoln's~~ sparrow
~~harris's~~ sparrow among ~~lewis's~~ woodpecker among ~~williamson's~~
    sapsucker among ~~clark's~~ grebe

~~wilson's~~ warbler among ~~wilson's~~ snipe among ~~brewer's~~ blackbird among
    ~~brewer's~~ sparrow
~~cassin's~~ finch among ~~steller's~~ jay among ~~say's~~ phoebe

with phoebe, my sister, i grow, animal among animals,
eye among eyes, gold leaf and clear glass,
tessera, tesserae, o little i let in this light

Wedding in America

I am dancing near the bank of the Little Spokane,
dancing with my brothers and sisters, the sky
darkening as we dance. Gold bursts
from the bride and groom, green shoots
through our bodies. We belt
Shut Up and Dance and *I Gotta Feeling.*
Ties, jackets, shoes tossed. Hips pop, arms
sway, weight thudding against cement
as we jump, stomp, spin. Someone starts a kick line
and we hold each other, dancing.
It is the electric breath of bodies
at home in their bodies that remains
when the couple runs through our tunnel of arms
and we all drive away.

At home, I check my phone:
Massacre in El Paso.
Out the window, the first fire of the season,
the night laden with carbon and water.
Mother prays for a shift in wind.
Sweat cools to salt on skin.
20 killed.
We were dancing.
In the morning, windows closed against smoke.
Another alert: *9 Dead in Ohio.*
Suspect's sister among victims.
Suspect shot down by Dayton police.
I am dancing with my brothers and sisters.
Near a dark shaft of river we are dancing.

Psalm Sleeping Between Circles & Lines

And God separated the light from the darkness.
                                        Genesis 1:4

How God's name divides (the wicked |
the righteous) the way my father and I
build a fence to keep the neighbor's knapweed
from our garden. To build a fireline, cut
and scrape vegetation till you reach mineral
soil, a strip wide enough to stop embers
from blowing across like seeds hungry to root
and feed. *Eventually the firefighters*
do prevail. Do *encircle.* Do *contain.* The edge
then felt with bare hands to find what heat
remains. Let no fire escape.

                              For a fire escape,
he hides a ladder under my bed | over the bed
a boy spreads paper hearts, red as the letters
I write   then burn out the window.

The Poet Forgets James 3:6

To write, I strike a match, tip the candle,
light the wick, the splint (taken from responsibly
managed FSC certified forests) shriveling—
a brittle black rope—then blow as the flame
stings my pinched fingertips (a sting like the switch
of a weeping cherry across bare thighs,
my body bent over a skirt). Sometimes
the stench of seared flesh. Sometimes a pagan
dance, threads of smoke following like a flag.

Once, I wake to an acrid haze, Cosmic
Cabin mixed with carcinogens, the flame eating
the tin base: formaldehyde and phalates. For days,
the trace of smoke and synthetic pine, the syrupy
ache of my head in the half-dark as I dream
my mother in the doorway shouting *Out! Out!*

Sonnet Starting with Arson

August 2015. When the smoke settles
in the city like sediment in a stream, my mother
buys masks, forbids us from opening windows,
the heat climbing through the old house to breed
in the attic where I sleep. An hour away
near Fruitland, a man dies trying to save his farm.
The ceiling drops, the sky so close I reach up
and choke God with one hand. *Thus men are held*
in the hand of God over the pit of hell . . . the fire
in their own hearts struggling to break out. The Forest
Service documents the success of Initial Attack
containing fires in Washington and Oregon. I
document the color of the sun cutting through
the haze, its eye unblinking, red as fish eggs.

The Poet Parses the Haze

How strange to be an *I*, to name on paper

the death we eat: smoke a mosaic of carbon

monoxide, particulate matter, and benzene.

Throats itch. Eyes sting. No absolute link

exists between exposure and non-traumatic

mortality. (The study can't separate

pollution from wildfire smoke in the state.)

The state line splits Lewiston and Clarkston along

the Snake river, the pulp and paper mills

spilling sulfur over the fields where I kick

and run in a red jersey before the bus ride back

to Spokane. In the mirror: the long cylinders

and buildings green as the oxidized Statue of Liberty,

the virgin wood impregnated, then bleached.

Virginity: A Chronology

16. He apologizes to my father for holding
my hand. 17. Not allowed to kiss, we
slip fingers between lips, spelunk soft fruit
while a movie splays blue light on his stubbly
cheek. 18. I defend the verse *suffer
not a woman to speak.* 1910. The Big Blowup
burns three million acres in the Northwest.
1935. The Forest Service decrees
every fire must be suppressed by ten a.m.
the following day. 1944. Smokey the Bear
bares his broad chest, wears blue jeans. 20-
20. I slip two fingers up the silt-soft
lumen between my double lips, raise them
milky with metaphor and sound.

Exodus

Metaphor: from the Greek *meta* denoting change

and the stem *to bear, to carry*, the way the plane carries

my body across the country from The Evergreen

State to Old Dominion, the way the Fairchild C-123

carries ammunition, evacuates the wounded, and sprays

Agent Orange over crops and trees. Fairchild: the name

of the air force base near Spokane where a gunman enters

the hospital in 1994, wounds twenty-two, kills four.

Agent Orange contains equal parts 2, 4-D and 2, 4, 5-T

which mimic the hormone auxin, spurring *rapid division*

in plant cells and *the uncontrollable growth of leaves, stems, and*

shoots. Uncontrollable: Between 1950 and 2010, the world

population increases by 174%. Climate change is projected

to increase vegetation productivity through elevated carbon

dioxide concentration and longer growing seasons, leading

to fuel accumulation in forests and *high-severity fires when drought*

and ignitions occur. The ecotones of ponderosa forests *may convert*

to grasslands or shrublands after these stand replacing fires,

regeneration decreased by moisture stress. When I exit

the airport in D.C., I bushwhack through humidity, a thicket

of chokecherry. In a warming climate, *loss of forests may occur . . .*

in the Northwest, particularly east of the Cascade crest. The US military

jokes during Vietnam, "Only you can prevent a forest."

As the West Coast Burns (IV)

The days mold and decompose. A banana peel fuses with yesterday's headlines, language complicit, complying.

Cardinals and bluejays screech outside my paned window, flashes of red and blue refusing my graph, my grid. My sight can't hold their movement. The news doesn't count the nonhuman among the dead.

*

One. The cicada on the laundry room floor. Its husk leaf-light on the lint-ridden linoleum.

Two. The raccoon reshapen into silly putty on the country road.

Three. The Swainson's thrush on the sidewalk, its cinder-black eyes burst from their sockets, tethered to the body by thin red threads.

What word culled you? In which language should i weep?

*

Something for your poetry, no?

*

Once, i dated a man who believed the earth is the center of the universe.

Is my lie any different: pulling distances into orbit as if naming is an act of gravity? The fantasy of *I*. As if their suffering is my suffering. As if i could speak for the trees.

Jesus tempts me, *Deny yourself.* Guilt and abstinence the first steps of healing. Let me employ the old theologies, incinerate self, sex, body. How easy to claim salvation, objectivity, entrance. What sweet seduction, this release from my own telling. Unburdened from an I, i fly and fly, cross country, story, species. (O Douglas fir, O big leaf maple, O Western hemlock darkening the hillsides from Portland to Eugene) i use the pronoun *you* and multiply. Am fern and frog and blackened mountain. A murmuration wheeling above the city like flakes of ash lifted by wind. For weeks we don't speak. My [   ] and i. My [   ] and—

*

Animal sounds echo at eight am. A dog like a seal in the stairwell. Pain and rage as paws screech across linoleum. Each bark a saw blade pulled across the morning's outstretched limbs.

How many mornings before i learn: in New Mexico, thousands of dead and dying birds. Swallows grounded on a golf course, bluebirds, warblers, sparrows, blackbirds. An *unprecedented* number. All insectivores, both migratory and year-round birds. The article states *some researchers suspect the West Coast's raging wildfires could be to blame.*

They could have been affected . . . They could have been forced to leave . . . They could have been forced into a longer journey . . .

*

What is a boundary but a threshold of responsibility, of return?

In the back of the canyon, a bush burns, a place of yearning not yet consumed. All this heat, and the bush will not pretend to be other than it is. A temporary city of matter, electrified by sap, gathered into bones and leaf. Spark plug, downed powerline, cigarette smoldering in dry grass.

My body won't be carried past where it exists.

*

What holds? The space past my cervix i fill with bones.

After Moving to Virginia, Alone

I don't know the names of these trees.
All broad-leafed, all bearded in ivy. Green
green green. A sheen of heat purples
the understory, each glass-backed leaf
a fractal of sun—clamor of chloroplast,
swell of cytoplasm. Unseen, cicadas spasm,
their tymbals buckling, unbuckling (O
agony O anticipation). After years pressed
under rust-red ground, this translucence,
these wings, the brothers shimmering into love
as they sing to sex August under an elm.
Shiver of web. Snap of twig. Nape licked
in sweat, I wade through hip-high weeds—
labia of light opening, opening.

The Poet Rethinks Her Profession

And the sonnet said *Let there be light*
and there was /laɪt/, a flick of the tip of the tongue
on the alveolar ridge, and *l i g h t*, a set
of symbols splintering toward a memory
of heat. Mourning, the atoms of animals
refuse to enter the ark I'm writing. What use
is another iambic line pleasuring the ear
of a single species? Choose your own reading
but I would have you believe the earthworm's
eyeless verse—how they ingest and excrete
the dark narrative of matter, their skin cells
listening for light and vibration. A gathering.
A division. There is no original expression,
only recycling, repetition.

This Belief, This Window

Sunrise gathers beyond my window: the bare
trees on the hill, the word *heaven* a question
on the sky's blank sheet. What is belief
but a room I fear to leave? Each morning,
a woman returns from her run and slowly
ascends the stairs, clutching her hip. Each morning,
I read wrestling and God in her limp, her body
a palimpsest for the patriarchs' myths.
The porch lights dim. Doors open. Sleepers
pass into the light and heat. A rooftop vent
flickers in the sun, exhaling exhaust behind
a holly tree, and for a moment I think I see
a small flame smoking among the branches,
the green untouched by the burning within.

Cognitive Dissonance

I touch my arm as if labelling a plastic box. I press a button; lungs breathe. On screen: a whale's innards laced with garbage bags and corrugated tubes. One way to view a sonnet is as a box or little room. How much can be packed inside before the body refuses? 48 pounds of plastic pulled from the dead mammal's stomach. Plates, nets, detergent packages still tattooed with barcodes. One way we cope with new information that conflicts with our beliefs is to convince ourselves that no conflict really exists. A crane lifts the body onto the bed of a truck. Trash blooms with blood over the lower lip. I swallow. I fit each new word inside the form passed down to me. The whale carries a fetus, the fetus already decomposed into a language my poems can't hold.

Limbo

I read love poems until the phone rings,
my mother asking as she has ever since I moved

away, *Are you reading scripture these days?*
Between the truth and my reply: a space

thin as a page. My mouth makes the routine
movements, bows into assent, bends

and straightens to row across sulphur
toward the shore where she waits for me

to land. Between the sound of the oars
and the circle of her arms, three eagles hover.

One breathing blood,
another fire.

Above both, the third wheels,
seeing everything as water.

Sightseeing in the Pandemic

Tallulah Gorge   white

         tulle drapes   in cascades

    an aesthetic release   the sign reads   the way my mother says

a better place when   my friend's father dies   how

words disguise   the water behind   the dam christened

    lake   pearly gates replacing   grief in the mind   I try to see

    what's   in front of me

        plastic   punctuating the

          green   phrases of

this hemlock and rhododendron   this   sluice   turbine   spillway

raised array of parallel lines   converting power from

    this water   when I say   *rage*

          I   see my friend's

    mouth   shaping

        God's name   six months after   when

  I say *river*   hands tear the concrete page

molecules roar   through right angles   water returns to water

            when I dream   no one tells me how

         to see   I wear

   another's face   the dead

I cradle   their throats

     my voice   honeysuckle

        entwined   with poison ivy

None of the music I know is for only one voice

Across the country, the old upright has grown
      stiff, untouched, untuned. My mother
reminds me of this. On the phone, she walks
      through the living room, past the dusty Steinway
she inherited from her great great grandfather,
      a music teacher who settled South Dakota
after the removal of the Sioux. Winter evenings,
      I'd sit on the squeaky mahogany bench
as families gathered around our woodstove,
      blue hymnals in hand, and wait for a voice
to call out a command—*All Hail the Power*
      or *Nothing but the Blood*. Outside the circle
of singers, I kept the rhythms and harmonies,
      led them through chorus and refrain, my fingers
guiding mothers and fathers up the mountain
      to *When We All Get to Heaven*. These days,
I stay awake asking who is included in "all"
      and my mother wakes at 3 to call
the ambulance, panic pressing against her chest,
      her heart breaking rhythm, breaking breath.
No one opens the piano now that I've left,
      its ivory keys chipped relics of a mammal
slaughtered into a symbol for the American
      middle-class. Around the fire, we never sang
of those outside the faith. It was never enough
      to build a room of sound so warm they all
called me *grace*. Sometimes, I fear my mother
      doesn't miss me, only the songs I played.

Self-Portrait as Diorama of a Room at Dusk

I have looked too long at the thin image
seen through the glass. The hour turns.
Vision begins to double back, a black
mirror dividing without from within. This is
what I've been. A figure in a shadow box,
a fixed shape in a red tableau. Table, chair,
throat, hand. A body I've only known
as sin. Lust buzzes outside: mosquito hum
in the dark, plastic shudder of the blue
porchlight. Hell is a lie I daily breathe,
here inside what still holds me. Yellow wings
of lamplight beat the back door, a bird
hurling its body against the glass. My face
looks back: a mask of shattered bones.

Nostalgia as Match Factory with Women Inside

from human urine and bone ash: phosphorus | phosphorescence | fossil | phoenix | phoneme | faux fur | fertilizers | fertility | fur baby | lay lady lay | lady lie | lye | lyric | lute | Lucifer | light-bearer | lightning | Zeus | Prometheus | god of fire | rod of fire | ring of fire | cast alive into a burning | Johnny Cash | my dad singing off key | basalt uplift of the Steens | ashen with spring snow | jackrabbits | sagebrush out the window | a window of time meaning | a frame I can't revisit | red phosphorus struck | a match | a flame | the window closing | through it: my escape

Awaiting the Apocalypse in Old Dominion

Past midnight, I unlock the door and walk
across the parking lot to a field circled
by asphalt and cherry trees. Four deer in the glare
of streetlamps, their tails white flames. Out West:
drought and fire in the forecast, spring snowpack
melting too fast, *severe* the adjective my sister
sends through the phone. Where is tomorrow
in this collage of clover and grass, the grass
Kentucky blue, a perennial introduced
by Spain, spread west by settlers, now naturalized
in all fifty states (the cultivar Cougar
bred in Pullman where I played basketball
after a man prayed, my body only a shadow
of the boys' glorious battle to come). How I prayed
for Christ's coming, two lions in my breast, the lamb
a tin of canned meat cutting the lip.

                                                the grass
the grass!   [as if] I can forget our invasion
of the continent   [as if] the blades are my sister's
hair
            the stars don't appear   their distant
fires smothered by stadium lights
                                                I rhyme
the animals into the dark   pairing
breath and death   how and
                                                        when

Sonnet with Dante, E.T., and Ted Berrigan

Whatever is going to happen is already happening.
No use speaking of circles when the inferno
is outside. To return, I'd need to expel
0.67 metric tons of CO_2, speeding
in an aluminum bullet across the country
to the state where I learned to disbelieve
in climate change, the state choking on smoke
as the climate changes. The pulpits say earth's end
is OK—we're alien as the long glowing finger
E.T. extends to Elliot's head. This is not
our home. All this territory extra, extravagant.
Let's dream of spaceships and sunsets clipping
the movie to a close as the man rides west,
ex nihilo, exiled, extracting the ecstatic.

Incantation for the Anthropocene

extract the exquisite corpse from the existential

exhume the exs and ohs   exxpose Exxon

exfoliate the eczema of the executive exchange

ex cathedra: an xfinity of exaltation and exhaust

ex silentio: extortion | exhortation

extra Ecclesiam nulla salus   excelsior!

excelsior!   the exiles explore eschatology

while the mine exudes uranium

                      excelsior!

explosives   exotic green rocks   excavated

on the reservation   excelsior!

exposure

x-rays

extirpation

As the West Coast Burns (V)

What does compassion mean across distance? Compassion from the Latin verb *to suffer* and the preposition *with*.

My faucet sputters, spits sound without form. Outside, men in neon maneuver yellow machines. The water cut off, a momentary need.

*

My mother visits the poem. She travels cross-country to sit with a notebook and pen and listen to the poem. She sits in a pew and waits for the poem to walk up to the podium. She waits for the poem to extrapolate the poem, to perform exegesis, exorcism. She waits for a man to carve three clean lines on the poem's skin and tell her where to stand.

She wants to know where i stand, the xy coordinate of my belief. i want to know the equation that will carry my body into the burning. i write water = water. i write ~~my~~ mother = the woman whose clothes burn off as she walks through fire. i write distance = the amount of carbon dioxide released when a machine travels the length of the vector from desire to need.

The page still blinks, motionless, the chasm between knowledge and grief. i lift a match to the polished wood behind which the poem stands, protected, in power.

*

After a fire, even if you have a house to return to, the water likely isn't safe to use.

What we see: a blackened car, *the melted skeletons of washers and dryers, a water pipe in the charred remains of a building.* What's hidden: contaminated plumbing, smoke and toxic chemicals pulled into the water supply. One such volatile organic compound is benzene, *which can cause nausea and vomiting in the short-term, or even cancer over time.*

Even if you don't drink the water, these compounds can be released into the air through washing your hands or showering.

Within the article, a photograph of a green hose surrounded by ash, its nose pointing left to right like the line of a poem read across space and time.

*

For four hours, i cannot shower, wash, or drink. The fast imposed by external force i read as solidarity, the way my mother reads scripture: extracting signs and symbols, matching her life to an established meaning.

When my mother asks how i make sense of why we are here, i don't answer. She keeps asking me questions, hoping she'll lead me to confess the god she says i need. i keep writing poems to reach her. Each of us trying to save the other in our own language.

*

Women kneel in skirts on the carpeted steps at the front of the church. Their faces fractal in the red glow cast down from stained glass. A pair of slacks straddles the podium. A pair of hands lifted over them. Each woman holds a child. A burnt or sin offering.

My therapist tells me i can change the dream. i start with a blue seam-ripper, dismember the clean tight stitches circling their waists. A miracle: i multiply the knives, one for each woman. Together we rend our clothes, rip collars and hems, tear cotton nylon polyester linen, the air clawed with our small violences, our bodies emerging—nipple, neck, mole, knee—like the knobs of mushrooms after a rain.

We strip till we are as bare as the woman who escaped the Beachie Creek Fire outside of Salem. i rend the words to reach her. Angela. The name of my aunt in Spokane.

*

My parents named me Hannah after the woman in the Bible. Hannah the woman who weeps and will not eat. The woman who disappears from the story after she gives birth to a son. Hannah the woman who prays so the priest cannot hear, her lips moving without sound. He thinks she is drunk.

*

Is this anger or grief? The need to resist the narrative that shadows me.

i want to write: This book was never about the fires. The story was never about the son.

*

In October, the news swerves to Colorado. Outside of Boulder, two mega-fires in the Rockies. My uncle's house bathing in smoke, my grandfather's bar pinned under an orange anvil. A resident says to the reporter, *It's crazy, just crazy. We'd usually be wading through snow this time of year.*

Drought and acres of trees killed by bark beetles. High winds. Record heat. The East Troublesome fire grows by 140,000 acres overnight. Smoke crowds the sky over the cul-de-sac where my mother pitched baseballs, grew breasts, walked to a field at the end of the street to see the horses gathered at the fence. It is here where we meet, two symbols in a coordinate caught between aspen and pine.

When we both reach out to touch the warm nose of a roan, our hands brush each other in the reaching.

*

Still, i eat but cannot weep. In my revision of the dream, i stand behind the podium and part my lips. My body opens. An O through which colors leap—rain, wind, thunder, fire, daughter—howling in a field surrounded by flames candling the trees.

Meet-Cute in the Anthropocene

under a field of vowels

you meet me

plastic bags drifting like petals across the blue page

a plaid blanket parsing the angles of my body

my body collecting crude oil drifting down from the trees

the trees the field where you meet me

and walk through consonants to wake

whatever remains of the sky the trees—

perhaps a hawk circling

Extended Sonnet with Turkey Vultures

inside the apartment complex, i practice belief in death
the way I once believed in god—the fall
from the balcony, the red bolt through the body,
then the holy emptiness, the self erased, cleaned.
six hawks in the distance, spiraling. turkey vultures
maybe. too far to see. the morning is a mirror
in which i do not recognize myself. carnivorous,
cadaverous. hidden litanies of death trailing everything
i name. i've seen the casualties of desire—scraps
of fur on october roads, bones and trash bleaching
in the weeds. chick-fil-a cup, rusted hub cap,
plastic sheetz bag. how to speak the word love
in a landfill. how to praise the body that continues
to eat. the ac hums, massaging the air, ferrying heat
away from me. at the bus stop, i tell myself i'm learning
to touch the shape of my life like the incised trunk
of the beech where a scarlet tanager sings

shureet shureet.

After the IUD insertion, i go camping in West Virginia

night by New River   a coal train

grates   against the dark's dull blade

blood   under a waxing moon
in the hollow between

two hillsides

i eat   chocolate

tongue   cherries   dip   a finger

in the dark smear of my body

viscous

metallic as
red clay

yesterday   a black snake   swallowed
a copperhead
on the sandstone bank

today
brown algae
and
wild raspberries
in the moon-mouthed porcelain

the bowl   a hunger
shadowed by my thighs

in the tent i wed my ache

my hips

two meteorites

embedded in the earth

On Seral Stages and Falling in Love

Somewhere between the languages we

became: a flame. The edge, the ecotone,

this broken line between the forest and

the plain, two spaces that bleed into each other

given fire, given time. How we circle

our unknowing, growing from herb to shrub

to tree, returning through fire, remembering

through fire all our words begin and end

with the grass. Let me loop back, let the blaze

undo this height. All my names for desire

have never kept my body clean. i will

not say *God* in this silence, this black soil

opened between us after we touch.

Poem in which i erase god's name from the New Testament

Somewhere along the way i remember the punishment

Somewhere along the way every dream becomes a simulation where someone won't let me leave until i dip a knife in Jesus's blood and kill the appropriate woman

Somewhere along the way i copy and paste Bible verses onto a shimmering white screen, then—*delete   delete   delete*

Somewhere along the way i begin to call these poems

Somewhere along the way the shapes of old/new systems moving toward me, fast, like buildings along a highway where i or someone like me was/is driving from the passenger seat with one hand

Somewhere along the way there is often a dive bar or a porch where i rewrite the night's metaphysics with the red stub of a cigarette i don't know how to smoke

Somewhere along the way i run out of change, out of language, and there is a toll, as there always is, at the bottom or top of the mountain

Somewhere along the way i let a man enter me on a porch by a river in a car on a picnic table under a blur of particular stars while particles of wildfire smoke burn my nose, bleed it

Somewhere along the way is always my mother

Somewhere along the way an empty Snapple outside a gas station becomes synonymous with water, with want

Somewhere along the way i dredge my body for the pattern of stresses in each book, chapter, verse

Somewhere along the way i do or do not pull the bag of Bibles from the back of my closet and drive across the country to the river of the city where i was born and

i am tearing each thin opaque page into fragments the size of the foam spitting over the falls

Along the way i stop needing the gesture, the erasure, the salvaging

i tell myself absence is also an epistemology

i tell myself ethics isn't only a god and his ghosts

Somewhere a man with a tattoo of a flaming angel on his bicep is stepping out of a Lana Del Rey song and telling me he's taking my name from the book of life

Somewhere along the way i let him

The Field of Particles Where i Fall

i'm in love with all the worlds that rhyme with *kiss*—in quantum physics

electrons only exist in interaction—little flashes in a field—little trysts

stolen within space and time—even a stone is a moment—a flickering

within a billion years—nothing remains equal to itself—nothing remains

together—*Who Wants to Live Forever?* Freddie Mercury sang five years

before he died of AIDS—O this whorl of light—this galaxy of tears and

lips where you slip from the bed to gather the morning—my fingertips

parse the space where you lay—

Religious Trauma

⟹ All rifles have mothers
⟹ Some mothers have daughters
⟹ Not all daughters are driven to Idaho in the rain

⟹ All language reduces to what's proven
⟹ How many times has your father said the word "broken"?
⟹ Some daughters touch themselves in darkness
⟹ Some daughters are wooden targets set out in the rain

∴ The form holds even when it's resisted
∴ Capitals, commas, subject-verb agreement
∴ Narrative, narrative, our holy omnipotent god
∴ You always hit the target, good daughter, your ears cupped in black
    muffs, body still and wet, your eye carving geometry into the rain

⟹ Some daughters are moving targets, red bullseyes stapled to their backs
⟹ Some daughters win certificates, are baptized *riflemen*
∴ These daughters are the same daughters

My father asks, "How do you define love apart from God?"

What's latent in the darkness.
Each sense that aids
remembrance. The light pulsing
beyond the names. Saltwater,
wind, sand, sun. Among
the four elements, my sister
and i a fifth, together something
close to spirit, howling
as we race toward the Pacific,
slick thighs stinging, vowels
unraveling to the sea. This is
the sound beneath the mountains:
a cry waking the i to receive

the pronouns of other species—
barnacles, gulls, sand
fleas, headlands
of shore pine and juniper,
salt marshes of elk and pickleweed,
basalt pools where my sister
and i poke pink and green
anemones. Memories blur
like bodies underwater: her voice
before, beside, behind me.
When do we first see the clear-cuts
on the Coastal Range? Love
opens the fault line under us.

The Lyric "I" Goes Shopping at Trader Joe's

"i" thinks this poem should begin with an image, perhaps a red pear or fiddle-leaf fig, something external with psychological resonance

"i" specifically wrote "fiddle-leaf fig" because yesterday "i" coveted this exact plant at Trader Joe's where dozens of plastic pots wrapped in green foil were arranged in neat rows in the store's open entrance

"i" plans on going to TJ's again today after finishing "i's" poem, in which "i" would like to make "i's" entrance subtly, in the 4th or 5th line, as an observer of a landscape or character in a narrative

"i" still believes "i" only deserves to appear in pastoral poems so that "i" can project "i's" experiences and emotions through the landscape without appearing to be self-obsessed

"i" knows that "i's" reluctance to write confessional poems is a product of "i" still believing at some fundamental level that to focus on the self is a sin

"i" doesn't quote-unquote "believe" in sin anymore though, of course, "i" is obsessively concerned with morality, primarily with the fact that "i's" apartment building doesn't provide recycling and "i" has been too lazy to drive "i's" paper bags of bean cans and egg cartons to a recycling center ever since "i" moved in over a year ago

"i" knows "i's" parents don't think "i" can have any moral foundation if "i" doesn't believe in God

"i" keeps forgetting "i" doesn't want to capitalize "god" anymore in "i's" writing

"i" personally thinks the word "believe" has as much meaning as the bag "i" fills with recyclable objects only to dump in the garbage bins in the building's basement at the end of the week

"i" knows that "i" tends toward religiosity, which "i" understands in a narrative sense, as in "i" grew up in a fundamentalist evangelical theologically reformed church-home-school environment and even after leaving, "i" still carries years of indoctrinated guilt and fear in "i's" body

"i" sometimes (ok, often) disassociates in TJ's, overwhelmed by choice and plastic packaging, each product a brightly colored mouth calling *Les Petites Carrots of Many Colors! Persian Cucumbers! Fresh Organic Cranberries! Teeny Tiny Avocados! Ricotta & Lemon Zest Ravioli! Unexpected Cheddar! Chili Onion Crunch! Crispy Crunchy Crisps! Spicy Porkless Plant-Based Snack Rinds! Amped-Up Almonds! World's Puffiest White Cheddar Corn Puffs! Maple Streusel Bread! Non-Dairy Pumpkin Oat Beverage! Honey Mango Shave Cream!*

"i's" first memory of disassociating is during potlucks in the basement of Christ Community Church, a low-ceiled room with linoleum floors where adults' voices echoed, overlapped, intertwined, a polyphony so loud "i" felt "i's" mind detach, grow small and cold, a marble "i" held in the pocket of "i's" dress, "i's" short body weaving in and out of clusters, escaping the well-meaning friends of "i's" parents, the teenage boys listening to i-pods at the corner table, "i's" mother's quick eye

"i" supposes "i" could make disassociation aesthetically interesting by calling it "negative ecstasy" in the poem but "i" is a bit disenchanted by aesthetics at the moment since "i" is haunted by the idea that beauty is merely a privilege or commodity only the wealthy can afford

"i" doesn't know why "i" continues to shop at TJ's when afterwards, "i" always feels incredibly exhausted and anxious because "i" can't stop seeing the invisible chemtrails wafting behind each item "i" unpacks from "i's" reusable grocery bags: the lives of the people who picked and processed the food, the emissions used to ship bananas from Ecuador, the plastics brewed from crude oil, the land stripped of nutrients from monoculture farming, fertilizer and pesticides running off from the fields into creeks and streams

"i" knows that "i" needs to resist making environmentalism "i's" new religion

"i" sometimes wonders if "i" left Christianity simply because believing in original sin and also realizing how "i's" actions are complicit in the climate crisis left little reason for "i" to exist "i" doesn't like to tell people that "i" wanted to die

"i" doesn't like to have to give a quote-unquote "reason" for "i's" decision to leave
Christianity

"i's" friend asked "i" the other day if "i" feels that there was a moment when "i"
unequivocally left Christianity or if "i" feels that "i" is still leaving to which "i"
replied that it feels like a long, slow untangling

"i" feels that creating a narrative to explain "i's" decision to leave Christianity is
manipulative and self-indulgent but this doesn't prevent "i" from doing exactly
that in order to somehow communicate to "i's" church-going family and friends
how "i" has moved from the "saved" to the "unsaved" side of the binary

"i" knows "i" was lucky to have mostly positive relationships during "i's" time in the
church

"i" feels guilty for betraying church people who were kind to "i" though "i" wonders
if the only reason people were nice is because "i" obeyed all of the rules

"i" thinks "i's" family thinks "i" had no legitimate reason to leave the church because
"i" did not experience abuse within the church

"i" knows being white, appearing straight, and performing articulateness gave "i"
privilege in "i's" church community

"i" knows "i" used piety and "i's" skill with language to gain respect and acceptance

"i" also knows "i" was sincere in wanting a relationship with god (whatever that
means) and in "i's" use of language to create a persona that matched what male
religious leaders told "i" "i" should be

"i" isn't interested in whether or not "i" was a quote-unquote "true believer" or just
someone very skilled at self-deception

"i" is mostly concerned with being a self these days as in

how to experience desire & pleasure

how to care for other living beings and the planet while also caring for oneself

how to have likes, dislikes, humor, anger, and boundaries without feeling guilty
for having likes, dislikes, humor, anger, and boundaries

how to return from TJ's with two bags of groceries without feeling guilty for
having money to buy organic produce when other people are hungry or
being worried about "i's" bank account balance because "i" bought organic
groceries and now has less than $50 until "i" gets paid or feeling disgusted
with "i's" self for being able to consume so much food in one week and
wondering if "i" would be a better person if "i" were not so dependent on
food for "i's" happiness

"i" is impressed by "i's" ability to simultaneously dislike the word "i" and use it
continuously

"i" isn't quite sure if this is a poem but "i" has worried too much about the edges
between binaries (heaven / hell) (human / nature) (prose / poetry) to now
worry about belonging to a single category

"i" is concerned, though, that this poem contains too much abstraction and not
enough imagery

"i" knows that "i" relies on imagery the way "i" relies on food and physical movement
to feel emotion

"i" experiences spells where "i" can barely feel affection for or intimacy with another
person

"i" is terrified of these silences

(while "i" has been typing this, the cat has jumped up on "i's" lap and demanded that
"i" move "i's" laptop to make space for his body

71

the cat doesn't give a fuck that "i" is composing metafiction about "i's" use of
   language and form and "i's" complicated relationship to "i's" own existence)

"i" thinks "i" can learn a lot from the cat, primarily not to take "i's" self so seriously
   and also how to ask for what "i" wants and how to say no to what "i" doesn't
   want

"i's" mother has asked repeatedly to read the book "i" is writing

"i" doesn't know how to tell "i's" mother that reading "i's" poems would break her
   heart by which "i" means she would be angered and grieved by "i's" anger and
   grief, by which "i" means that "i's" mother would believe that "i's" deconstruction
   of Christianity and "i's" discovery of "i's" sexuality are proof of "i's" descent into
   darkness and sin

"i" doesn't know how to convince "i's" mother that "i" is actually happier than "i"
   has ever been but "i" does know how to end this poem, to give it a sense of
   completion and satisfaction

in the poem, "i" can experience a sense of return by repeating the reference to
   Trader Joe's where, in the poem, "i" is currently buying salt, pepper, bananas,
   garlic, parsley, a yellow onion, Yukon gold potatoes, green lentils, and baby
   spinach

in the poem, "i" doesn't have to worry about "i's" parents ever reading this

in the poem, "i" can have enough money in "i's" bank account to buy or not buy the
   fiddle leaf fig

A Middle-Class Pastoral

i
know a pine
near the place
where the marmots mate
we could spread a blanket in its shade
we could listen to the tussle of squirrels
the groan of traffic
we could lie so still the ants would touch us
would walk on our skin as if it were the earth
& the birds would share their voices but never their names
still i'd ask & in your saying
i'd look at your face
see two suns through green needles
near the train tracks near the chain fence
near the grass crumbed with clover near asphalt
always near asphalt
i know a pine
limbs lopped off by saws
stout with centuries, transplant or native
still we could lie & i'd unbutton my body
i'd say
here is
my body
near
your body
near
the place
where
the marmots
yes
the marmots
still
the marmots
come
to mate

An Apostate's Abecedarian

All fall i complain to you about the light. Two days
before the solstice, the optometrist explains the irregular
curve of my eyes. *Astigmatism* he says but i think *stigmata*:
desire converging to a point of pain on a saint's
exalted palms or feet, the sudden bloom of blood from
francis's side mirroring the wounds of his beloved christ. In
giotto's painting, beams of light extend from a
hovering crucifix through the kneeling francis as
if his body is just another window, a glass frame for
joy and sorrow to pass through. i never
knew the word *miraculous* even when i still
longed for a shadow i called lord to touch
me in the night. In the new year, you and i climb the cliffs
near summersville lake, your body above me in a blur
of opaline light. My neck cranes back, rope
passing between my hands as you ascend, the sun's
quiver piercing my eyes. Why this grief as you
rise away from me? Ice breaks open on the lake's blue
sheen. In the painting, gold rods pin his body into place,
thanks the saint's only reply. What ties us together is wholly
unholy: a dirty green rope knotted at our hips. i am
vicious and infested with vice. My vision muddies
when you bite my neck under the dark's stars and signs, your
sex pressed to my pelvis where god never came.
Yes, every second a supernova explodes. Some
zeal asks for pain in the absence of touch. Even at its
zenith, can tenderness say *enough?*

Ode to the lowercase "i"

little walker   shy interrupter   quiet tally of time and heat   pen's
familiar brush and flick   black moon above a seaside cliff
ubiquitous finger   thin mirror refracting light   eager apprentice of
my body (one body among many others   not standing above)   first
word before *love*   last letter in *bikini* and *tsunami* and *fungi*   i   i   i
dear candle   dear signpost   dear sounding rod   how you pull me
toward shadow soil stone   touch water flame   (mold mouth into *fire*
call vowels together in *rain*)   stem   stamen   occasional stick-in-the-
mud   slippery eel always lunging from my throat   almost a semi-
colon   a pause between two melodies   this tight seam weaving   you
to we   and yes   no atom ends   one world becomes another   each
pronoun a stream   we cross   to reach   beyond

As the West Coast Burns (VI)

It is late and early in the story of my coming of age.

i flip through the notes i wrote at the start of the year before the pandemic, before sex, before apostasy, before the West's pyrotechnics and lightning. In my journal, a diagram of forest succession drawn with circles and dotted lines. Each sphere a snapshot of an ecosystem at a point in time, arrows signaling the direction of growth in the absence of fire:

grass/shrubs → seedlings/saplings → young trees → mature trees → old growth forest

In the presence of fire, the pathways splinter, depending on the severity. Does it burn the crown or only the understory? A low-intensity fire can regenerate a forest's current seral stage, but a lethal fire resets the pathway, the community looping back to grass and herbs.

What path have you taken, little i, falling from your height to sprout in this field, a single stem among the plural iiiiiiiiiiiiiiiiiiiiiiiiiiiiiiiiiiiiiiiiiiiiiiiiiiiiiiiiiiiiiiiiiiiiii of bunchgrass, blue gama, and elk sedge?

*

Of my doubt, my father says, *God doesn't change even when the world does.*

Of my deconversion, my mother says, *Perhaps you never knew God's grace. Perhaps you were never truly saved.*

i write and erase a face in the window, the face i once addressed with a capital *I*. Does it matter whether the letter is *I* or *G*? How many times did i pray while looking in a mirror, needing an image i could address, a body i could believe?

*

On a walk, i see a hawk with a broken wing on my neighbor's doorstep. *You shall love your neighbor as yourself* . . . Too easy of a metaphor. He hops away from me.

Hawk from the Proto Indo-European root *kap-*, meaning *to grasp*. i google "cooper's hawk" and am shown the website for a winery. What figure of speech is this: a word stolen from its referent, relocated, and extorted for economic profit?

i try Wikipedia (free, but they're asking for donations) and find a description that matches my already hazy memory of the bird. i can never identify a species at the moment of our encounter. Wasn't it Augustine who said we can never name the present? For as soon as we say "now," it has already passed, the words fading into the space where something has disappeared or changed.

*

As climate change and over a century of fire suppression lead to more high severity fires in the future, it could be harder for forests and other ecosystems to recover, *Science Magazine* reports. *Already, some ecosystems in North America that have had frequent or intense burns are not regenerating. In some places, such as the sagebrush ecosystem of the Great Basin west of the Sierra Nevada mountain range and forests in the Klamath Mountains along the California-Oregon border, invasive shrubs or grasses appear to have taken over.*

As for the aftermath of this year's fires, it's hard to predict. *Some habitats will bounce right back, others will struggle for years to recover what was lost, and still others will completely change to a new type of habitat.*

*

O this liturgy of the literal, this forest where i dwell, where i write a forest for my thoughts to sit among bark, humus, lichen, leaf. When i was a girl, i climbed the maple in our backyard, pressed my ear against its trunk, and heard the wood groan and creak as wind tossed the canopy.

O little i, i set fire to the images i thought i knew, and what grew back from the ash? Here i am listening as i did long ago, listening to the trees.

As if i could speak for the trees.

The word "tree" is problematic / And trees, being inanimate #notreally // Aren't the kind of thing you sleep in. / They're the kind of thing you #burn

Over centuries, a single fungus can cover many square miles and network an entire forest. The fungal connections transmit signals from one tree to the next, helping the trees exchange news about insects, drought, and other dangers.

if the name nearest the name / names least or names / only a verge before the void takes naming in, / how are we to find holiness, / our engines of declaration put aside, / helplessness our first offer and sacrifice

Between 1800 and 1900, the nation burned its forests into the atmosphere, then turned to digging fossil forests from the ground.

Turns out we've polluted the woods / With prophecy, . . . / . . . I intellectualize nature too often // Using rhetoric to suggest a narrative / When there isn't one

. . . when trees are really thirsty, they begin to scream . . . at ultrasonic levels.

Your species can't say it / You have to do spells & tag them

Don't colonize that tree by naming it a nameless poet said Lucky he doesn't have to hunt for his food / a naming poet said

Thus, large conventional power plants today are burning fossil forests. . . . Today, hardly any coal is being formed because forests are constantly being cleared, thanks to modern forest management practices (aka logging).

But I'm cursed.

I then imagine / Myself—from nature's POV—as host / To a virus that materializes in the lungs / And exists through the mouth, an infection / We call language.

. . . language . . . lies on the borderline between oneself and the other. The word . . . is half someone else's.

The branches / Make a sound like . . .

only in the interweavings . . . / does reality hold // to a single face its name

Matins

A candle to light the morning,
purpled weekend want,
his body sleeps,
my body reads
California's burning.

Under the force of meaning
the threshold flickers. Guilt's familiar
alphabet stirs beyond the door.

Riven this way all language aches
with the taste of our trespasses—
his tongue, my clit, those nights pluming the jeep
with carbon and sweat, windows wet with news
of Death Valley's record heat.

Have you held mercury
in your mouth? Have you
tasted the rod of glass,
its shape syntactical and cold?

i was taught to pray
but not the words to praise the nearness
of his face. How to fold distance in half,
how to press together the edges
of destruction and love?

Your pen is
plastic. It will melt when
you ask it.

i held the narrative until
the narrative held me back,
girdled my body, cut cells
down to sapwood. Each word
i trace incinerates: pyrography of skin.

Tell me when the ash gathers
on your eyelashes, tell me
the name you call when all is effigy:
a photograph of a house swarmed
with flaming swords.

Not yours, not yours.

Fire Map: California, Oregon, and Washington

historic | histrionic | this season at least 40 people at least 7,000 structures at least five million acres at least | initially | with more than | over a month | though it is now | ___% contained | hysteria: *originally a (supposed) physical disorder of women attributed to displacement or dysfunction of the uterus, characterized particularly by a sensation of fullness in the abdomen and chest, with choking or breathlessness* | research suggests | smoke hazardous | hazard: *a gambling game complicated by a number of arbitrary rules* | air quality index: a measure of how healthy, how clean | unclean: in Leviticus, anyone who touches a woman during her bleeding | what do you call the red leaking out of me | red stains on the map | blooming like the black mold in the corner of my ceiling | the key: red = active burning | brown = land burned since the beginning | of August | my grandmother texts me: *I'm feeling very sad tonight because the three states I've lived in and loved all my life are burning | so much loss of forest | people and animals* | my father prays for his mother's peace | pax americana a tax a pox an ax to tree and tree and tree | hysterectomy | this excision | ordered by officials after a gender reveal ignites four-foot-tall grass east of LA after | a mother loses her unborn child and her one-year-old son trying to outrun the flames after | she stumbles toward the Columbia in the dark | her husband holding her son | her body a season without water | warming

A Short Catechism

What is the chief end of hands?
To glorify hips and to enjoy their surrender.

What rule hath hips given to direct us how we may glorify and enjoy them?
Have you asked? Have you listened?

What are hips?
*Hips are two bones, largely composed of star-shaped cells, joined together with cartilage
at the pubic symphysis, which comes from the Greek preposition "together" and the
root "to be, grow, exist."*

Are there more hips than one?
The light of the body is a candle with two wicks.

How many persons are there in the hips?
*As many bees are in a hive, as many tongues are in a bear eating eggs and honey from
the hive, as many times the bear is stung by the bees, their hive torn open by the
bear's blunt teeth.*

How doth hips execute their decrees?
How does the moon push and pull the sea, how does a planet orbit into an eclipse?

How did hips create hands?
The hand guides the hand into the hips—

like this.

When we met, we were being paid

to clear an old mining trail in the New River Gorge,
our machines hoisted on our khaki shoulders

when we stopped for tulip poplars and the hard
nubs of unripe blackberries. i'm telling this story

to remember the gas canister that leaked through
my backpack into my skin, to remember the beech

limbs i lopped, the fallen trees your saw cleaned up
through division, the heart-shaped trillium

my weed-eater ate in the name of conservation,
spewing shards of plastic into the ferns

as the nylon strings whacked stones, roots,
and stems. A summer of looking and then

the whispered collision of our bodies
in the dark: a heat held in the fist

of my air-conditioned apartment, air purchased
from Dominion Energy and powered by

the combustion of long dead organisms that once
fucked and bloomed as we do—with breath,

with bodies. i cannot write the word *love*
without writing *oil, axle, engine*, without naming

the machines we use to cross the distance
of desire. The vector of ecstasy runs on 13 mpg,

your old Jeep huffing over the Appalachian
Mountains. i'm told, again, by science

that the best thing i can do for our planet is
to not bear children. i'm told by the doctor

that an IUD may increase my pain and bleeding.
i'm told by my father that capitalism works

because human nature is bent toward greed.
Still i dream of an animal feeding at my breast,

the copper T inside me almost the shape
of the pickax i used to hack roots on the trail

above the old coal mine. Still there is that word
love in flashes when you drive four hours to visit

and we lie in my big white bed. For hours i forget
the fires, our emissions. For hours i cradle

the illusion between us: when we touch,
we are the only ones touching.

Woman who escapes Santiam Fire on foot loses her mother and son to the flames

Angela Mosso, her mother Peggy Mosso
and her son, Wyatt, in an undated photo.
Angela   her mother
            and her son   in an undated
photo.   her mother   and
her son   in
            Angela
            in a   photo.
      her   and her
                                    and
her son.
            Peggy   and   Wyatt,   a
      dated photo. A   mother
                        un

She   watched   nowhere
spread   She had
                  come out of
wildfires come out of   where
and
    nowhere
      out of   swiftly
            out of   spread

She had watched
                  if   survive
      She
            knew
                  ultimately   knew
                                    choice

            She had to
            She had to leave
            She had to leave her mom behind

            a road once   familiar now shrouded by smoke

      a road once
            a   road
                  now
      a   woman
            shrouded by smoke
                                    a road
                        what looked like a   woman
                        once   but now shrouded by
            almost

                              who's   missing
She   knows
She   knows
She   knows

Litany to Be Recited by My Hands

your hands	a book we name together: honey locust
honeysuckle	ears bit open for
my hips	black walnut
blackberries	the dark seeds of
sun on your chest	black-eyed susans
quartz	clearings
where the scalpel	of ox-eye daisies
quarried skin	asterisked
licked	with chicory
white	thickets of
laurel	rhododendron
open above	fern-fronds where i hold
the repetition	humus of bone & stem
humming your limbs	under the poplar

A Brief Lesson in Rimming

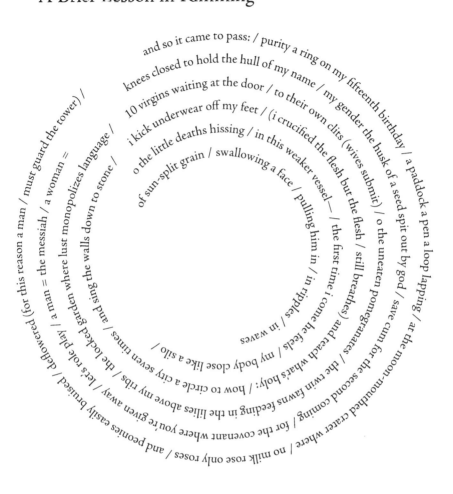

and so it came to pass: / purity a ring on my fifteenth birthday / a paddock a pen a loop lapping / at the moon-mounted crater where you're given away / lets role play / the locked garden where lust monopolizes language / (for this reason a man / must guard the tower) / a man = the messiah / a woman = / deflowered / and peonies easily bruised / and sing the walls down to stone /

knees closed to hold the hull of my name / my gender the husk of a seed spit out by god / save cum for the second coming / for the covenant where you're given away / no milk rose only roses /

10 virgins waiting at the door / to their own clits (wives submit) / o the uneaten pomegranates / the twin fawns feeding in the lilies above my ribs / how to circle a city seven times /

i kick underwear off my feet / (i crucified the flesh but the flesh / still breathes) and / reach what's holy: / the lilies above my ribs /

o the little deaths hissing / in this weaker vessel— / the first time i come the feels / my body close like a silo /

of sun-split grain / swallowing a face / pulling him in / in ripples / in waves

Only a Quarter of Species May Survive the End of the Century

we go to / a sieve / in / go to sea / rising / you and i in a / the cross-stitch / language / you and / empty the atmosphere / uniform learning the names / sea in / a sieve we / the water / acidifying / song / a sieve / of wires we call / i with a thimble to / of CO_2 / you and i in / of trees / each name an ark built / by a man with an ax / everyone knows it was Noah's wife who asked the animals inside / as if one pair could save a species from extinction / as if the men hadn't already hunted whole families to oblivion / you are a man from a family of hunters / you wear your hair long and know how to weep / you call to confess the baby bat that fell when you hit a rotting tree / i call to read poems about the land / where i first loved you: fog lifting / from the green mountains snaked / with highways and diesel trucks / a Trump sign on a clear-cut / YES COAL billboards / cigarette butts / floodplain of possum skulls and baby doll limbs / a bottle of brown piss tucked under mist-slicked rhododendron / rock snot and algae blooms invading Bluestone Creek / hollers and holiness on Heritage Road / sandstone seamed with coal / purple lightning over the river / deer grazing on the grass where we dumped dishwater / (are you reading out loud yet? / is there a voice in the room?) / in a room, i dream of what's outside / you are cutting down trees to build a trail / i am weaving a net / the minutes slip through

broad-winged hawk

polyphemus moth

southern-running pine

chicken mushroom

smooth alder

american beech

eastern dobsonfly

orange milkweed

red-spotted newt

Forty miles south of my parents' house, a wildfire decimates the small town of Malden and consumes thousands of acres of wheat

becoming witness

was not

enough

outside the ash-filled foundation of what was once

i've seen   loss   i've

corkscrewed

split
off

this wildfire season has been
        the signals of climate change

the future

a blackened brick shell
        nearby

i wish i

returned

why

save

I

fire

spells   end   spells   beginning

space   creates

others

As the West Coast Burns (VII)

An elegy for the endangered Columbia Basin pygmy rabbits, half
of their population baked or asphyxiated in the Pearl Hill Fire this
September.

A hymn for the wood-boring beetles that sense heat from miles away
and swarm burnt trees in the hours after a fire, seeking charred wood in
which to lay their eggs.

An elegy for the sage grouse, for the 30–70% killed in the flames, for
the sagebrush they inhabit east of the Cascades, a shrub-steppe habitat
that's shrunk 80% since the 19th century.

A hymn for the black-backed woodpecker that dines on the wood-
boring beetles' larvae and drills nesting cavities in fire-damaged forests.

An elegy for the mule deer whose charred carcass twists like a piece of
driftwood in the photo taken 60 miles west of where i was born.

A hymn for the chickadee and the mountain bluebird, for the Myotis
bat and the flying squirrel who live in the cavities after the woodpeckers
leave, their excrement dispersing seeds that grow into pine grass and
fireweed.

An elegy for the eight porcupines unable to escape the Whitney fire
that razed the Swanson Lakes Wildlife Area. An elegy, here, in the
wetlands of a poem, for their bodies found in what had been an oasis of
rushes, cottonwood, and aspen.

A hymn for the after-life, for the uncertainty of what will grow in the
decades after burnt trees topple, sky to soil, their trunks now providing
shelter for rodents and snakes.

An elegy for the fires suppressed through dogma and the government's
zealous crusades. An elegy for the fire deficit haunting the West, its
stockpiled fuels erupting into infernos that burn hotter each year.

A hymn for the mosaic of burned and unburned land after a fire, a black and green checkerboard that protects animals and regenerates a habitat.

An elegy for the loss of these mosaics as fires become larger and more severe, refugia and pyrodiversity replaced by monochrome moonscapes of bones and ash.

A hymn for the matches first made from human bone and urine, an elegy for the bodies that became sites of flame.

A hymn for my father who taught me how to lite and tend a fire, for my mother who taught me to sit near a body in pain.

An elegy for the sounds i made before syntax, before story.

A hymn for the match i hold to the page.

A hymn for the silence after my words have burned away where i find myself crying and can't say whose water is released, which river splits the stone inside me.

Mist rises from the falls in the center of the city where my mother wakes and sleeps. After a season of fire and smoke, she walks through the pines, pulling me into her orbit of praise and grief.

Notes

In writing the poems for *Rain, Wind, Thunder, Fire, Daughter*, I've begun to conceive of language as a kind of fungal network in a forest through which trees exchange vital nutrients and information. The sources and supplemental information that follow are evidence of this ecological practice, through which I acknowledge my indebtedness to and interdependence with the texts and writers whose work I've drawn from.

Definitions and etymologies come from the Oxford English Dictionary and from etymonline.com, except where otherwise noted.

The book's epigraph is from *Green-Wood* by Allison Cobb. Copyright © 2010 by Allison Cobb. Used by permission of *Nightboat Books*. All rights reserved.

Invoke | Revoke

The wildland-urban interface, or WUI, "is the zone of transition between unoccupied land and human development. It is the line, area or zone where structures and other human development meet or intermingle with undeveloped wildland or vegetative fuels." "What Is the WUI?" *U.S. Fire Administration*. Accessed January 31, 2024. https://www.usfa.fema.gov/wui/what-is-the-wui.html.

Forty-four percent of the United States is considered wildland-urban interface, and of that percentage, about 220 million acres (an area twice the size of California) is at high risk of wildfire. More than one third of the U.S. population lives in the WUI, and since 1990, the WUI has continued to grow "at the astonishing rate of 3 acres a minute, 4,000 acres a day, 1.5 million acres a year." Ferguson, Gary. *Land on Fire*. Portland, OR: Timber Press, 2017.

A research study that analyzed wildfire records from 1992–2012 found that, nationwide, 84 percent of wildfires were started by humans; however, the statistics differed for the Pacific Northwest. In Idaho, for example, humans caused only 31 percent of fires, while in Oregon, Montana, and Washington, humans were responsible for 48,

53, and 70 percent of ignitions, respectively. The study concluded that the "Pacific Northwest's lower numbers are due in part to population density: Especially in Idaho, there are millions of acres of uninhabited or sparsely populated land." Landers, Rich. "84 Percent of Wildfires Caused by Humans, Study Finds." *Spokesman-Review*, February 27, 2017. https://www.spokesman.com/blogs/outdoors/2017/feb/27/84-percent-wildfires-caused-humans-study-finds/.

As the West Coast Burns (I)

Fuller, Thomas, and Giulia McDonnell Nieto del Rio. "As the West Coast Burns, Communities Unravel With Each Death." *The New York Times*, September 12, 2020. https://www.nytimes.com/2020/09/12/us/wildfire-deaths.html.

A Power Comes Up Between the Voices

The title is excerpted from a line in Brenda Hillman's poem "The Arroyo." Hillman, Brenda. "The Arroyo." In *Loose Sugar*, 13–15. Hanover, NH: Wesleyan, 1997. © 1997 by Brenda Hillman. Published by Wesleyan University Press and reprinted with permission. All rights reserved.

Italics are excerpted from 1 Timothy 2:11–14: "Let a woman learn quietly with all submissiveness. I do not permit a woman to teach or to exercise authority over a man; rather, she is to remain quiet. For Adam was formed first, then Eve; and Adam was not deceived, but the woman was deceived and became a transgressor" (English Standard Version).

A Poem Changes Nothing

The title is excerpted from a line in Brenda Hillman's poem "Economics in Washington." Hillman, Brenda. "Economics in Washington." In *Practical Water*, 51–53. Middletown, CT: Wesleyan, 2011. © 2009 by Brenda Hillman. Published by Wesleyan University Press. Used by permission. All rights reserved.

After warriors from Palouse, Couer d'Alene, Spokane, Yakama, Pend d'Oreille, Flathead, and Columbia tribes defeated Colonel Edward Steptoe in 1858, the U.S. Army sent Colonel George Wright on a punitive military expedition throughout Eastern Washington. Wright's orders from the army stated, "You will attack all the hostile Indians you may meet, with vigor; make their punishment severe, and persevere until the submission is complete." After Wright defeated the allied tribes at the Battle of Spokane Plains, the Spokane Chief Garry approached Wright to discuss a treaty, to which Wright responded by threatening the tribe with war and extermination if they resisted submission. Over the next month, Wright took hostages and hung, without trial, a total of seventeen indigenous warriors on the suspicion of their involvement in the deaths of two miners at Fort Colville. As the army marched upriver toward the Idaho border, they set fire to lodges and food supplies and killed 690 horses belonging to the Palouse. In a letter to General Clarke, Wright remarked on the damage, "A blow has been struck which they will never forget." Cutler, Don. "Your Nations Shall Be Exterminated." *Military History Quarterly*, Spring 2010.

In December of 2020, the Spokane City Council voted to change Fort George Wright Drive to Whistalks Way to honor Whist-alks, the wife of the Yakima chief Qualchan and a Spokane warrior who helped to resist Wright in 1858. Dodd, Amber D. "George Wright Drive Changes to Whistalks Way, Honoring Female Warrior Whist-alks: 'We Finally Got It Done.'" *Spokesman-Review*, August 20, 2021. https://www.spokesman.com/stories/2021/aug/19/george-wright -drive-changes-to-whistalks-way-honor/.

Sonnet Ending in People's Park

From its headwaters in the Rocky Mountains, Latah, or Hangman, Creek flows through Latah County in Idaho before meandering northwest toward Spokane. Latah County was established in the Idaho Territory in 1888 after a committee headed by William J. McConnell coined the word "Latah" by combining the Nez Perce words La-Kah and Tah-ol. The committee gave the word the meaning of "place of the pestle and pine." Monroe, Julie R. *Moscow: Living and Learning on the Palouse*. Charleston, SC: Arcadia, 2003.

The controversy surrounding the creek's name began when Colonel Wright hanged, without trial, the Yakima Chief Qualchan and six other Palouse warriors near the creek after taking them as hostages under the pretense of a truce. In memory of this crime, locals began to use the name Hangman Creek, and the name continues to appear on maps, despite multiple attempts by federal and county governments to standardize a single name.

Wood | Word

A *spiritual feeling* refers to: "Large ponderosa pines with yellow bark invoke a sense of a majestic forest and spiritual feeling in people who frequent these forests." Graham, Russell T., and Theresa B. Jain. "Ponderosa Pine Ecosystems." In *Proceedings of the Symposium on Ponderosa Pine: Issues, Trends, and Management, 2004 October 18–21, Klamath Falls, OR*, 1–32. Albany, CA: Pacific Southwest Research Station, Forest Service, U.S. Department of Agriculture, 2005.

The Latin name became— / unusually among trees—the common name is quoted from the *Spokesman Review*. "Ponderosa Pines: Towering Giants." *Spokesman-Review*, February 12, 2018. https://www.spokesman.com/stories/2018/feb/12/ponderosa-pines/.

Animalia

This sonnet's use of brackets was inspired by *American Cavewall Sonnets* by C. T. Salazar.

Rain, Wind, Thunder, Fire, Daughter

The title is taken from Act 3, Scene 2 of Shakespeare's *King Lear*, in which a raving Lear calls out to the storm: "Nor rain, wind, thunder, fire are my daughters. / I tax not you, you elements, with unkindness. / I never gave you kingdom, called you children. / You owe me no subscription."

Now a little fire . . . here / comes a walking fire is excerpted from the following scene where the Fool tells Lear, who is stripping off his clothes, "Prithee, nuncle, be contended. 'Tis a naughty night to swim in. Now a little fire in a wild field were like an old lecher's heart—a small spark, all the rest on's body cold. Look, here comes a walking fire."

Nearly 85 % of wildland fires are human is adapted from "Nearly 85 percent of wildland fires in the United States are caused by humans." "Wildfire Causes and Evaluations." National Parks Service. *U.S. Department of the Interior.* Accessed January 31, 2024. https://www .nps.gov/articles/wildfire-causes-and-evaluation.htm.

As the West Coast Burns (II)

Italicized language in the sections beginning with "i read, *Human activity causes . . .*" and "*By the end of the century . . .*" is quoted from the *New York Times.* Schwartz, John, and Veronica Penney. "In the West, Lightning Grows as a Cause of Damaging Fires." *The New York Times,* October 23, 2020. https://www.nytimes.com/interactive/2020/10/ 23/climate/west-lightning-wildfires.html.

Prophet | Profit

Italics are excerpted from Revelation 8:7: "The first angel blew his trumpet, and there came hail and fire, mixed with blood, and they were hurled to the earth; and a third of the earth was burned up, and a third of the trees were burned up, and all green grass was burned up" (New Revised Standard Version).

Sonnet with a Mouth Full of Dollar Bills

"*Ponderosa / pine fuel[s] the economies of the West beginning / in the 1860s*" is quoted from "Ponderosa Pine Ecosystems."

Mapping the Channeled Scablands

The Channeled Scablands is a region in Eastern Washington characterized by dry falls, coulees, cataracts, potholes, streamlined hills, and giant current ripples as a result of the cataclysmic Missoula Floods during the last ice-age. The large boulders that litter the sagebrush and grassland—also known as glacial erratics—were rafted in on icebergs in the massive floods, their granite and argillite rock types conspicuously out of place in this region of basalt bedrock. In describing this startling landscape, Glenn Hodges points out the "pattern of braided channels" in the scablands that mirror the crisscrossing pattern water creates after a rainfall or a flooding river—just on a much larger scale. Hodges, Glenn. "Formed by Megafloods, This Place Fooled Scientists for Decades." *National Geographic*, March 8, 2017. https://www.nationalgeographic.com/history/article/channeled-scablands.

A Ponderosa Pine Reader

During World War II, the U.S. government claimed that information about ponderosa pine forests was "vital to the conduct of the war and to any plans for our postwar welfare." Cowlin, Robert W., Philip A. Briegleb, and F. L. Moravets. *Forest Resources of the Ponderosa Pine Region of Washington and Oregon*. Washington, D.C.: U.S. Dept. of Agriculture, Forest Service, 1942.

As the West Coast Burns (III)

The sky was red and the moon was up is quoted from the *Spokesman-Review*. Epperly, Emma, Rebecca White, and Chad Sokol. "Eastern Washington slammed by fires, dust storms, and power outages." *Spokesman-Review*, September 8, 2020. https://www.spokesman.com/stories/2020/sep/07/eastern-washington-slammed-by-fires-dust-storms-an/.

Double Sonnet with My Shirt Off

The definition of basal area is taken from the Forest Inventory and Analysis Glossary, published online by the Forest Service. https://www.fs.usda.gov/research/understory/forest-inventory-and-analysis-glossary-standard-terminology.

Bridal | Bridle

Italics are excerpted from 1 Corinthians 7:9: "But if they cannot exercise self-control, they should marry. For it is better to marry than to burn with passion" (English Standard Version).

Psalm Sleeping Between Circles & Lines

Italics are quoted from the National Park Service. "Wildland Fire: Fire Construction." National Park Service. *U.S. Department of Interior.* https://www.nps.gov/articles/wildland-fire-fireline-construction.htm.

The Poet Forgets James 3:6

James 3:6: "And the tongue is a fire, a world of unrighteousness. The tongue is set among our members, staining the whole body, setting on fire the entire course of life, and set on fire by hell" (English Standard Version).

"FSC" stands for the Forest Stewardship Council, which certifies timber products that have come from "responsibly managed" forests. However, an article published by the Yale School of the Environment reported that the label of "FSC" has become another method of greenwashing, sometimes sanctioning logging practices that are often illegal and environmentally destructive. Additionally, FSC certifications have been, in the overwhelming majority, awarded to forests in the northern hemisphere, which does little to affect the rapid pace of tropical deforestation occurring in countries of the global south. Conniff, Richard. "Greenwashed Timber: How Sustainable Forest Certification Has Failed." *Yale Environment 360*, February 20, 2018. https://e360.yale.edu/features/greenwashed-timber-how-sustainable-forest-certification-has-failed.

Sonnet Starting with Arson

Italics are quoted from Jonathan Edwards' notorious sermon "Sinners in the Hands of an Angry God."

Narrative Timeline of the PNW 2015 Fire Season. Edited by Tim Sexton. United States Department of Agriculture, 2016. https://www.govinfo.gov/content/pkg/GOVPUB-A13-PURL-gpo90659/pdf/GOVPUB-A13-PURL-gpo90659.pdf.

The Poet Parses the Haze

Doubleday, Annie, Jill Schulte, Lianne Sheppard, Matt Kadlec, Ranil Dhammapala, Julie Fox, and Tania Busch Isaksen. "Mortality Associated with Wildfire Smoke Exposure in Washington State, 2006–2017: A Case-Crossover Study." *Environmental Health* 19, no. 4 (2020). https://doi.org/10.1186/s12940-020-0559-2.

Spokane houses the headquarters of Clearwater Paper, the manufacturer that owns the pulp and paper mills in Lewiston. Clearwater supplies more than half of the store brand toilet paper, paper towels, tissue, and napkins to stores in the United States. It also makes bleached paperboard used for commercial printing and packaging (appearing in products such as milk cartons, cereal boxes, paper plates, and paper cups). Conifers are preferred for making the pulp used in paperboard because of their longer cellulose fibers.

Virginity: A Chronology

Italics are excerpted from 1 Timothy 2:12: "But I suffer not a woman to teach, nor to usurp authority over the man, but to be in silence" (King James Version).

Exodus

Italics beginning with *"rapid division"* are quoted from *Green-Wood.* Cobb, Allison. *Green-Wood*, 80. New York: Nightboat, 2018.

From "Climate change is projected . . ." to *east of the Cascade crest,* information is paraphrased or quoted. Halofsky, Jessica E., David L. Peterson, and Brian J. Harvey. "Changing Wildfire, Changing Forests: The Effects of Climate Change on Fire Regimes and Vegetation in the Pacific Northwest, USA." *Fire Ecology* 16, no. 4 (2020). https://doi .org/10.1186/s42408-019-0062-8.

As the West Coast Burns (IV)

Something for your poetry, no? is quoted from "The Colonel" by Carolyn Forché. Forché, Carolyn. *The Country Between Us,* 16. New York: Harper and Row, 1981. Copyright 1981 by Carolyn Forché. Used by permission of the poet. All rights reserved.

Italics in the fourth section are quoted from the *New York Post.* Eustachewich, Lia. "Thousands of dead birds in New Mexico could be linked to West Coast wildfires." *New York Post,* September 15, 2020. https://nypost.com/2020/09/15/thousands-of-dead-birds-in -new-mexico-could-be-linked-to-wildfires/.

The Poet Rethinks Her Profession

The *dark narrative of matter* is a riff on a phrase from Brenda Hillman's poem "A Geology." Hillman, Brenda. "A Geology." In *Cascadia,* 7–14. Middletown, CT: Wesleyan, 2001. © 2001 by Brenda Hillman. Published by Wesleyan University Press. Used by permission. All rights reserved.

Nostalgia as Match Factory with Women Inside

This poem refers to the songs "Lay, Lady, Lay" by Bob Dylan; "Lady Lie" by Rainbow Kitten Surprise; and "Ring of Fire" by Johnny Cash, respectively.

The phrase "cast alive into a burning" alludes to Revelation 21:8: "But the cowardly, unbelieving, abominable, murderers, sexually immoral, sorcerers, idolaters, and all liars shall have their part in the lake which burns with fire and brimstone, which is the second death" (New King James Version).

Sonnet with Dante, E.T., and Ted Berrigan

The first line is a quote from one of Ted Berrigan's sonnets. "Sonnet L" from *The Sonnets* by Ted Berrigan, edited by Alice Notley, copyright © 2000 by Alice Notley, Literary Executrix of the Estate of Ted Berrigan. Used by permission of Viking Books, an imprint of Penguin Publishing Group, a division of Penguin Random House LLC. All rights reserved.

The term *ex nihilo* is Latin for "out of nothing" and refers to the Christian doctrine that the universe was created by God from nothing, not out of preexistent matter, and that it is absolutely dependent upon divine power for its existence.

Incantation for the Anthropocene

Exxpose Exxon launched in 2005 as a campaign to shed light on ExxonMobil's dangerous environmental politics. Rex Curry with Greenpeace reports that Exxon has "known since the 70s about the causes of climate change and the dangers climate disruption poses," yet between "1998–2014, Exxon gave over $30 million" to groups that deny climate change. Curry, Rex. "Exxon's Climate Denial History: A Timeline." Greenpeace. Accessed January 31, 2024. https:// www.greenpeace.org/usa/fighting-climate-chaos/exxon-and-the-oil -industry-knew-about-climate-crisis/exxons-climate-denial-history -a-timeline/.

The Latin *ex cathedra* literally translates as "from the chair" and refers to the Pope's authority to speak infallibly about Christian doctrine or morality.

The phrase *ex silentio* is Latin for "from silence" and refers to when an argument is made based on lack of contrary evidence.

The Latin phrase *extra Ecclesiam nulla salus* means "outside the church, there is no salvation."

Excelsior is Latin for "ever upward" or "higher."

In 1954, Jim and John Lebret, two brothers from the Spokane Tribe, discovered uranium on Spokane Mountain and opened Midnite Mine, run by the Dawn Mining Company, "a subsidiary of the multi-national mining company Newmont Corp." McDermott, Ted. "Deb Abrahamson blames mining pollution for her cancer, keeps fighting toxic legacy on Spokane reservation." *Spokesman-Review*, December 1, 2019. https://www.spokesman.com/stories/2019/dec/01/deb-abrahamson-blames-mining-pollution-for-her-can/.

Over the next 27 years, "more than 3 million tons of uranium ore and 33 million tons of waste rock were blasted out of the hillside of the Spokane Indian Reservation." The mine brought jobs and money to the reservation, employing around 500 tribal members at its height until it closed in 1981. Workers were given inadequate safety protections and often carried ore dust home on their clothes to their families, unknowingly exposing them to radiation. Cleanup of the radioactive debris and a pit of "eerily blue water" did not begin until 2016 and is due to be completed by 2025. Meanwhile, water with high levels of uranium and other toxic metals has been poisoning the reservation's watershed for almost seventy years, leaking into Blue Creek which flows through the reservation before emptying into the Spokane River, then eventually the Columbia. Tribal members have repeatedly reported unusually high rates of cancer, and the EPA has concluded that someone who gathered plants, hunted game, and drank water from the area would have a 1-in-5 chance of getting cancer. Apple, Charles. "Midnite in the Garden of Good and Evil." *Spokesman-Review*. Accessed January 31, 2024. https://www.spokesman.com/stories/2019/dec/02/midnite-mine-radioactive-uranium-mine/

As the West Coast Burns (V)

Italics and information about water contamination are taken from *The New York Times*. Horberry, Max. "After Wildfires Stop Burning, a Danger in the Drinking Water." *The New York Times*, October 2, 2020. https://www.nytimes.com/2020/10/02/science/wildfires-water-toxic.html.

"It's crazy, just crazy. We'd usually be wading through snow this time of year" is quoted from *The New York Times*. Brennan, Charlie and Jack Healy. "In Colorado, It Feels Like a Fire Season Without End," *The New York Times*, October 23, 2020. https://www.nytimes.com/2020/10/23/us/colorado-wildfires.html.

On Seral Stages and Falling in Love

In "Ponderosa Pine Ecosystems," Graham and Jain explain how seral stages progress in a ponderosa pine forest: "Succession is a term applied to the gradual supplanting of one community of plants by another on a given site through time. Vegetative complexes evolve after a disturbance such as a lethal fire. . . . Early-seral stages often begin with a grass/forb/shrub stage, succeeded by tree seedlings and saplings which grow to young trees, and subsequently develop into the late-seral mature and old vegetative complexes. In some systems, such as those dominated by ponderosa pine, these or similar stages may develop in less than 250 years but in other systems, such as Pacific coastal Douglas-fir . . . it may take in excess of 1,000 years for the full compliment of structural stages inherent to the system to develop."

The Lyric "I" Goes Shopping at Trader Joe's

This poem was inspired by "The Lyric 'I' Drives to Pick up Her Children from School: A Poem in the Postconfessional Mode" by Olena Kalytiak Davis, published in *The Poem She Didn't Write and Other Poems*.

As the West Coast Burns (VI)

See note about forest succession for "On Seral Stages and Falling in Love."

In *Confessions*, Augustine writes, "Therefore, if the present, so as to be time, must be so constituted that it passes into the past, how can we say that it is, since the cause of its being is the fact that it will cease to be? Does it not follow that we can truly say that it is time, only because it tends towards non-being?"

Italics in the fourth section are quoted from *Science Magazine*. Pennisi, Elizabeth. "As wildfires continue in western United States, biologists fear for vulnerable species." *Science Magazine*, September 30, 2020. doi: 10.1126/science.abf0544.

The phrases *where i write a forest for my thoughts to sit* and *i set fire to the images i thought i knew* are riffs on lines from Sara Nicholson's poems "Let Them Think I Am No Different" and "O'er," respectively. Nicholson, Sara. *What the Lyric Is*, 44–48, 76–77. The Song Cave, 2016. Copyright © 2016 by Sara Nicholson. Used by permission of the poet. All rights reserved.

As if i could speak for the trees

This poem is a collage of the following sources:

Ammons, A. R. "Coast of Trees" and "Givings." In *A Coast of Trees*, 1, 46. New York: Norton, 2002. Copyright © 1981 by A. R. Ammons. Used by permission of W. W. Norton & Company, Inc. All rights reserved.

Bakhtin, Mikhail. "Discourse in the Novel." In *The Dialogic Imagination: Four Essays*, 259–422. Translated by Caryl Emerson and Michael Holquist. Edited by Michael Holquist. Austin, TX: University of Texas Press, 1981.

Cobb, Allison. *Green-Wood*, 30, 104. New York: Nightboat, 2018. Copyright © 2010 by Allison Cobb. Used by permission of Nightboat Books. All rights reserved.

Hillman, Brenda. "Practical Water" and "Hydrology of California." In *Practical Water*, 4–6, 85–95. Middletown, CT: Wesleyan, 2011. © 2009 by Brenda Hillman. Published by Wesleyan University Press. Used by permission. All rights reserved.

Nicholson, Sara. "Now That's What I Call Music," "The Lamp of Beauty," "Adjuncts," and "The Archaeology of Private Life." In *What the Lyric Is*, 9–15, 38, 54, 55–57. The Song Cave, 2016. Copyright © 2016 by Sara Nicholson. Used by permission of the poet. All rights reserved.

Wohlleben, Peter. *The Hidden Life of Trees*, 10, 48, 94. Translated by Jane Billinghurst. Vancouver, BC: Greystone Books, 2016.

Fire Map: California, Oregon, and Washington

This poem was written in response to *The New York Times'* interactive online map of the same name.

A Short Catechism

This poem repurposes questions from The Westminster Catechism.

Woman who escapes Santiam Fire on foot loses her mother and son to the flames

The text of this poem repeats and erases sentences from an article reporting on the 2020 wildfires in Oregon. The title is my own. Lynn, Capi. "A desperate rescue: A father's heartbreaking attempt to save his family from a raging fire." *Salem Statesman Journal*, September 10, 2020. https://www.statesmanjournal.com/in-depth/news/2020/09/10/oregon-wildfires-santiam-fire-evacuations-leave-family-members-dead/5759101002/.

A Brief Lesson in Rimming

This poem was inspired by "How (Not) to Speak of God" by Mary Szybist, which appears in her book *Incarnadine*.

Forty miles south of my parents' house, a wildfire decimates
the small town of Malden and consumes thousands of acres of
wheat

The text of this poem is an erasure of a *The New York Times* arti-
cle. The title is my own, as well as any changes in capitalization.
Morlin, Bill and Mike Baker. "Wildfires Bring New Devastation
Across the West." *The New York Times*, September 9, 2020. https://
www.nytimes.com/2020/09/09/us/fires-washington-california
-oregon-malden.html.

As the West Coast Burns (VII)

Goldfarb, Ben. "The Loss That's Killing the West's Wildlife." *The
Atlantic*, September 30, 2020, https://www.theatlantic.com/
science/archive/2020/09/wests-wildfires-are-killing-off-its-wildlife/
616549/.

Landers, Rich. "Wildlife, habitat take devastating hit from wildfires
across region." *Spokesman-Review*, September 21, 2020. https://
www.spokesman.com/stories/2020/sep/20/wildlife-habitat-take
-devastating-hit-from-wildfir/.

Maggiacomo, Taylor. "Life After Fire." *National Geographic*, March
2021.

Mapes, Lynda V. "Endangered wildlife, habitat burned in Wash-
ington wildfires; years of effort to boost populations wiped out."
Seattle Times, September 16, 2020. https://www.seattletimes.com/
seattle-news/environment/endangered-wildlife-habitat-burned-in
-wildfires.

Acknowledgments

This book exists because of infinite small and large gifts. If you are read-
ing this, you are one of them. Thank you for coming close, into this space
of encounter. I have been touched and transformed by more people than I
can name—thank you to everyone who has shared life with me, even for
a little while. These poems would not be possible without you.

Ongoing gratitude to Claudia Keelan, Andrew S. Nicholson, and
the other editors of the Test Site Poetry Series for believing in my
poetry. And to the entire team at the University of Nevada Press for
your care and patience while creating this book. There's an eleven-year-
old child somewhere spinning in circles because you've made her dream
come true.

To all my writing teachers and mentors over the years for feeding
my obsession, and especially, always, to Bill Jolliff. You once told me that
poetry is a space where I don't have to be theologically correct. Thank
you for giving me permission to hear myself.

Everyone at the University of Virginia's Creative Writing MFA—Rita
Dove, Kiki Petrosino, Debra Nystrom, Lisa Russ Spaar. Thank you for
sharing your generous, expansive minds. Barbara Moriarty, your presence
is love itself. Brian Teare, the only advisor this book could have had. For
initiating me into ecopoetry, for continually challenging me to find what's
underneath. You see me so well.

Enduring love to my community of writers and friends. Jake Bienve-
nue, Lucas Martínez, Sophia Zaklikowski, Kate Cart, Gahl Pratt Pardes.
These poems are deeply indebted to my peers in workshop whose feed-
back and presence have taught me so much: Andy Eaton, Mary Clare
Agnew, Anita Koester, Betsy Blair, Michelle Gottschlich, Hajjar Baban,
Henrietta Hadley, Katherine James, Madeline Miele, and Wheeler Light.
Most of all, to my poetry cohort, for being with me through everything,
for loving every person I've been. Raisa Tolchinsky, Jeddie Sophronius,
Kyle Marbut, and Hodges Adams. Tenderness and respect and awe for-
ever. Hodges, your friendship is tough and true. I would do it all over
again, except for the fleas.

To my family. This book has always been for and because of you.
Nana and Papa, thank you for providing me with the space and love

I needed during the first few months of the pandemic to write these poems and run in the Blue Ridge mountains. Grandma Sue and Joanie, for always being in my corner. Aunt Angie, for showing me how to hold together anger and compassion. David, Phoebe, Ruthie, and Dan—my brave, big-hearted siblings, you are everywhere in these pages, even when you're not named. All we share delights and sustains me. To my father, for your tenderness, for teaching me to play with words and listen to trees. To my mother, for your fierce, relentless love.

Gratitude to the editors of the following journals in which some of these poems first appeared, often in slightly different forms:

About Place: "Double Sonnet with My Shirt Off" and "A Feminist Field Guide"

Arkansas International: "Genesis," "A Power Comes Up," and "A Poem Changes Nothing"

Cutbank Literary Journal: "Fire Map: California, Oregon, and Washington"

Dogwood: A Journal of Poetry and Prose: "When we met, we were being paid" and "Only A Quarter of Species May Survive the End of the Century"

Great River Review: "Extended Sonnet with Turkey Vultures," "An Apostate's Abecedarian," and "A Brief Lesson in Rimming"

Interim: "Wood | Word," "Psalm Sleeping Between Circles and Lines," "Sonnet with a Mouth Full of Dollar Bills," "Sonnet Starting with Arson," and "Forty miles south of my parents' house, a wildfire decimates the small town of Malden and consumes thousands of acres of wheat"

Nimrod International Journal: "I Place My Mother in a Scripture" and "Phonics"

Permafrost Magazine: "As the West Coast Burns"

Willow Springs: "Eve Speaks of Her American Childhood"

About the Author

H. G. DIERDORFF earned her MFA from the University of Virginia. She is the recipient of the 2022 Dogwood Literary Award for poetry, the 2022 Daniel Pink Memorial Poetry Prize, and a Vermont Studio Center Fellowship. Her writing has appeared in journals such as *Cut Bank, Arkansas International, About Place,* and *Willow Springs.*